$18.95

THE
AMERICAN
UNIVERSITY

THE
AMERICAN
UNIVERSITY

problems
prospects
and
trends

edited by
JAN H. BLITS

Prometheus Books

700 East Amherst St. Buffalo, New York 14215

In commemoration of the
University of Delaware's
sesquicentennial
1833-1983

Published 1985 by Prometheus Books
700 East Amherst Street, Buffalo, New York, 14215

Endpaper engraving, "Old College Hall, 1870" courtesy of the University
of Delaware Archives.

Contents

v

Preface

The essays in this volume were written and compiled to mark the University of Delaware's 150th anniversary. The essays by David S. Saxon, Richard L. Venezky, Virginia B. Smith, and John B. Slaughter were originally delivered (in slightly different form) at the university's sesquicentennial convocation held in Newark, Delaware, September 29–30, 1983. While the occasion for this collection is the celebration of one university's history, the concern of the volume is the future of American universities as a whole.

The volume focuses on issues and trends relating to science and technology, liberal education and the aims of the university, and academic governance. The first group of four essays, discussing the university's response to the demands of an increasingly technological society, takes up questions concerning science education and research. Saxon and Slaughter explore the development and economics of university research as well as the place of science education in the larger university curriculum. Howard E. Simmons and Alan McClelland examine the inherent promise and peril of evolving industry-university research relationships, while Venezky analyzes the dramatic implications of computer technology for altering many aspects of academic life.

The second set of three essays is concerned with the fundamental character and objectives of undergraduate education. Smith addresses the need to reevaluate and expand the role of liberal education in an era emphasizing technical and preprofessional training. Jan H. Blits examines whether liberal education belongs in the modern research-oriented university; and Frank B. Murray, assessing recent reports on the effectiveness of American schooling, suggests the relevance of the reports' findings to higher education.

The last two essays discuss the contribution of administration to the well-being of the university. C. Harold Brown, Linda Tom, and Eric Brucker argue for a tough and careful reexamination of university governance to meet the challenge posed by nationwide trends of declining enrollments and fiscal cutback, and each essay indicates possible directions for the future. The afterword by John A. Munroe highlights the University of Delaware's 150-year history.

Many people were generous in devoting countless hours to planning the university's 150th anniversary celebration. On behalf of the entire university community, I express deep gratitude to Dr. Samuel Lenher, Chairman of the Sesquicentennial Advisory Committee of the Board of Trustees, and to the members of his committee, Elbert N. Carvel, G. Burton Pearson, Jr., the late Preston C. Townsend, Board Chairman J. Bruce Bredin, Catherine Flickinger, J. Allen Frear, and Harold Schmittinger, for their advice and guidance in all phases of planning and preparation. I am also grateful to everyone who served on the Campus Support Committee and Cultural Subcommittee for their unstinting efforts in both initiating and reviewing proposed projects. I also thank all the members of the Convocation Committee, chaired by L. Eudora Pettigrew and C. Harold Brown, for planning the convocation and related symposia. Also deserving words of acknowledgment are those individuals who contributed to the preliminary planning under the direction of G. Arno Loessner. Special thanks go to the faculty, students, alumni, professionals, staff, and friends of the university, too numerous to name, who helped make the celebration a notable success.

Special recognition and thanks are also extended to Jan H. Blits for editing this book and to Kathleen C. Blits for making additional editorial suggestions.

E. A. Trabant
President, University of Delaware

David S. Saxon

Science and Liberal Education: What Lies Ahead

This essay is an attempt to look ahead to the future of the American university and, more specifically, to consider in that view the place of science in liberal education.

Now to look ahead, we must know where we are coming from and identify the most salient features of the landscape. I start with three dominant facts about our society: it is technological; it is xenophobic; and it is nuclear. Its technological character means that everyone needs to know something about the nature and limits of science. It also means that we must give our scientists and engineers a knowledge of human history and human values, and an understanding and appreciation of values other than those inherent in a purely technological perspective. These ends must be fundamental educational goals in our future.

The xenophobic character of our world—the prevalence of mutual suspicion and fear among people of different cultures and nationalities—means that the potential for conflict is constant and profound. We will never diminish this potential until we find ways of overcoming the barriers of race and nationality, of educating ourselves about each other. That goal must also be a high priority for the university, and for all of education. The third characteristic of our age—its nuclear capability—makes it urgent for us to address the other two.

11

Our time, of all times past, is peculiarly and particularly an age of science and technology. Science is our great intellectual adventure. In its technological character, our society and our world are on an accelerating and irreversible track; inevitably, they will become more and more technological. These developments have had, and will continue to have, a profound influence not only on university science, but also on the very shape and size of the American university.

The origins of the unprecedented growth and productivity of university science over the past four decades can be traced to the Second World War, and in two senses. First, harsh political repression in Europe before and during the war led to a large influx of brilliantly talented scientists into the United States—Einstein and Fermi, Von Neumann and Bethe, and others—whose pioneering scientific work helped to establish the United States as an international center of research and development. Second, the contributions of new kinds of scientific knowledge and skills—in nuclear physics and solid-state physics, for example—turned out to have direct, immediate, and critically important applications to the war effort. The Manhattan Project is just the best known example.

Because basic science and the applications it made possible proved to be absolutely vital to our survival, many people became convinced that it was essential to the national interest that a framework for systematically encouraging support of science be established when the war had ended. The man who sketched out that framework was Vannevar Bush, former chairman of the Massachusetts Institute of Technology, who proposed in his famous report entitled *Science, The Endless Frontier* that the federal government underwrite basic research—and that meant university research—on a scale undreamed of before.[1]

Bush's proposal was the first step toward the establishment of a new and spectacularly productive partnership between universities and government. I believe that this alliance will continue to be of paramount importance even though the federal government's support of basic research in the universities has ebbed somewht for a variety of reasons—some having to do with the economic troubles of recent times and some with other kinds of strains that have developed in the relationship. While these recent trends have led many—too many—to view the future of American science, and of the American university, with anxiety, even with despair, I am not among them.

On the contrary, I am optimistic. One reason is that the support of university science continues to be strong—indeed, by any previous standard, enormous—although from cycle to cycle, and from field to field, there will always be some ebb and flow. Another reason for optimism about the future is the fundamental health and the inherent quality of the basic research performed in this country. When I talk to Japanese visitors, for example, I am often struck by just how keenly they feel the difference between their capabilities for performing basic research and ours, and by how economically vulnerable they consider themselves as a result of their relative weakness in this area. Throughout the whole of my professional life, American universities have been the major source of new discoveries, of new understandings of nature; and there is no reason, barring a failure in will, that this scientific leadership should not continue through the end of this century and into the next.

In fact, I believe that we stand on the verge of remarkable and perhaps unparalleled developments and opportunities in our research—that we stand, as the phrase goes, at a hinge of history. What lies ahead? In my own field of physics progress will, I believe, continue at an accelerating pace as each new understanding builds upon the next—in the physics of elementary particles, solids, and materials as well as in astrophysics and cosmology. In mathematics, I expect rapid exploitation of the recent breakthrough in the realm of the nonlinear which, until now, has been largely beyond our reach. And in the two extraordinary fields of biotechnology and information technology, I see—to put it baldly—such a staggering capacity for change and innovation as will transform our world, physically and intellectually, in ways beyond imagination.

It is tempting to go beyond these broad statements, to see if we can spell out the exciting potentialities with some degree of specificity. But it is safer to speak in general terms of the intellectual ferment that is bound to characterize the years ahead; safer simply to recognize that university programs, departments, and centers inevitably will have to reflect and accommodate in one way or another the transformations and changes which lie ahead. No doubt it is quite safe to predict, in particular, that the trend toward bigger-than-ever science, which means also toward more expensive-than-ever science, surely will continue and that the consequences just as surely will be large. For example, in the field of elementary particle physics there presently seems to be broad support within the community for the construction of a huge 20-TeV (trillion electron volt) proton superconducting collider, measuring perhaps 20 or 30 miles in diameter, which will cost approximately $3 billion. The great NASA Space Telescope now being built, to take another example, will engage in one university center, astronomers from 22 universities and institutions, including the European Space Agency, and will require $1.1 to $1.2 billion, excluding launch costs.

The cost and scope of such enterprises are clearly beyond the capacity of single institutions and, increasingly, even of single countries. As a result, the implementation of such efforts often depends on new kinds of organizational arrangements, which are becoming more and more interinstitutional and international in character. Such science, in short, will not be a cottage industry.

Even without reference to these very large-scale enterprises, the cost of science is bound to increase because of the growing complexity and sophistication of instrumentation coupled with its computerization and automation. While the remarkable ongoing development of instrumentation extends the reach of our research and improves productivity, it does exact a price. The rising costs of research, although skewed to science, are not peculiar to it. Consider, for example, the insatiable demands of that great core facility, the library. One solution for the easing of these and other costs surely must lie in the cooperative and creative sharing of resources, both between institutions and, what surprisingly is often harder, within institutions. I believe that in the years ahead we will of necessity have to encourage and require more sharing, including that of the greatest resource of all, our faculties.

All these developments will have an important infuence on the evolution of our academic programs and on the ways in which we educate our students, not the least of which are our graduate students. In some fields the research mode is no longer that of a professor and a few students. Instead, a modern experiment may be carried out by a large team in which the student, quite typically, plays only a modest supporting role. How in that circumstance do we help him hone his own creative edge, strengthen his self-reliance, and develop his own intellectual style? How in particular, given the enormus cost of some of today's experiments, do we provide that essential of learning, the freedom to make mistakes?

Besides these problems of scale, others arise from the accelerating advance of knowledge and the rapid rate of development of new programs and even entirely new fields. Such changes will create their own requirements for the flexibility of our universities and, what is even more important, for the flexibility of our faculties. As our universities grow, should we keep adding new fields without end, without displacing some of the old? If fields become obsolete, do people? And if some faculty do not adjust and adapt to changing requirements, what should we do about it?

While in some ways university science is changing in scale and becoming bigger than ever, in other respects it continues to be decentralized and performed in a broad array of institutions. Located throughout the land, and engaged in modes both of cooperation and competiton, these institutions have endowed the university scientific enterprise in America with unparalleled vigor and resiliency. The rich diversity of our institutions is an important source of strength. It has meant, in particular, that we are not committed to any one way of accomplishing our aims, whether they be educating our young people or fostering research. Out of that diversity has come a readiness and a capacity to experiment, to innovate, to take and accept risks in devising new arrangements that will surely serve well the requirements of the future. There are characteristics we should and, indeed, must seek to preserve.

The capacity to experiment and innovate must also be mar-shalled more effectively in the service of liberal education, a longstanding concern of our colleges and universities that must continue to occupy a significant place in the future of American higher education. Moreover, we must carefully consider the role of science in a liberal education. Let me begin with the question: What does it mean to be a liberally educated person? To look at the history of the idea is to be struck, as one examines the changes in the aims of education from Plato and Aristotle to Newman and Arnold and on to the debate of our own day, with the difficulty of articulating its meaning. But I see at least one continuing thread in the fabric of liberal education that provides a constant over the years. Liberal education has always attempted to reflect what a particular society thought was important to know and to under-stand at a particular time. It represented society's collective wisdom about the skills and knowledge a person needed in order to be at home in the world and to make the best use of and derive the greatest pleasure from whatever talents he or she possessed.

This is still true today, although we are far less confident than the Greek or medieval philosophers about exactly what these skills are and what the knowledge ought to be. In the earlier days of western civilization, the elements of a liberal education were an-chored quite solidly in absolutes from Aristotle and from theology that changed only slowly, even imperceptibly, over the years. To-day, as I have suggested, the rate at which our knowledge of the physical world evolves creates for us an age in which change itself is a deeply signifcant fact. As a consequence, like everything else in our culture, our ideas about liberal education reflect this fact, with its accompanying and pervasive fragmentation and uncertainty.

Further, if relevance to its own time is one essential of a liberal education, it follows that science and technology have wrought so many changes in the way we live and perceive the world that no educated person can afford to be ignorant of the character and limits of science; no person demonstrating such ignorance can be called educated. Yet the state of general scientific knowledge in this country is dismal. Our scientific and technological illiteracy is so pervasive that the great majority of otherwise educated, intelligent, and inquisitive people are quite unable to bring informed judgment to bear on almost any question connected with science and technology. This failure of fact and of relevance is a failure of liberal education in our time.

More specifically, what we have failed to teach a majority of our students, including many of the most highly educated, is that science is neither a mystery for the few nor a haphazard collection of facts. It is, on the contrary, a highly unified and consistent view of the world. We should be able to give our students the understanding that science is built on a foundation of general laws that link together various observations about the physical world and provide a framework within which various potentialities, facts, and theories can be evaluated. Further, it should be possible to convey to students not only the power but also the limits of general scientific laws, even if these young people do not intend to master the sciences to the degree necessary to permit them to use the laws of nature. I believe most strongly that this kind of broad understanding of science is an essential element of a modern liberal education.

I want to stress also that it is equally essential to give students of science, engineering, and other professional studies a proper sense and appreciation of the contributions that have been made by humane learning. Liberal education should provide a sense of the richness and complexity of creativity in the humanities, and of how that kind of creativity concerns itself not so much with the measurable and quantifiable aspects of the world as with the universals of human experience. Students should be able to understand how the humanities seek to explore not only the rational but the other dimensions of human nature, and they should be able to see patterns and connections in our experience that are no less real and no less significant than those revealed by science. Liberal education should also include an understanding of how we evolve out of and are affected by our history, even if that history cannot be understood in terms of the paradigm of continuous progress familiar to science. The study of the humanities should help science students understand the limits of rationality as well as its powers and, in addition, should help them to recognize the enormous difficulty of making judgments involving questions of value, even though the very process of living forces us inescapably to do so.

To achieve these ends and in so doing provide the basis for a modern liberal education is the outstanding challenge to contemporary education. And as with any worthy challenge or goal, there are difficulties and barriers. A principal obstacle science students face in coming to an understanding and appreciation of the humanities is their own perhaps unconscious arrogance toward nonscientific studies. The dazzling success of science in revealing and harnessing the powers of nature has given it enormous prestige in our century, a prestige that is in many ways entirely deserved. But the other side of this phenomenon is that the complex of beliefs and attitudes associated with scientific knowledge is in danger of overshadowing and diminishing other equally important kinds of learning. Regrettably, science and engineering students have all too many opportunities to pick up from those further along in the profession the attitude that nonscientific or prescientific thinking is fuzzy and somehow inferior because it does not conform to the canons of scientific rigor—and is thereby second-rate and second-choice.

The arts student, on the other hand, is confronted with the rapidly growing complexity of science and with the fact that science is written in a special language, the language of mathematics. It is a simple fact that as knowledge and understanding progress, as scientific investigation concerns itself with almost unimaginable extremes of space and time and energy, science describes a universe that is ever more remote from daily experience and thus ever more difficult to comprehend. That is why, in the words of the late philosopher Charles Frankel, science is an "inaccessible language" for most people.

This tendency to inaccessibility is made worse by the unfamiliarity of most people with enough mathematics to understand science. Almost everyone would agree that student deficiency in mathematics presents a difficult obstacle to the science teacher. Some, like the Nobel physicist Richard Feynman, believe the obstacle to be absolute. Says Feynman: "The strange thing about physics is that [in order to express its] fundamental laws we need mathematics. The more laws we find, and the deeper we penetrate nature, the more this disease persists." And he adds, "It is too bad that it has to be mathematics, and that mathematics is hard for some people. Physicists cannot make a conversion to any other language. If you want to learn about nature, to appreciate nature, it is necessary to understand the language that she speaks in. She offers her information only in one form."[2]

While Feynman is surely right in the most pure and fundamental sense, I do not believe that an appreciation of science as a proper part of a liberal education requires that kind of grounding in mathematics. William Fretter, a former colleague at the University of California, and I wrote a physics text in which the mathematics was restricted to elementary algebra and geometry; it provided "verbal explanations . . . for those students for whom mathematics hinders, rather than aids, understanding of the physical principles."[3] While this effort failed to fulfill our hopes, it was not because of the role and treatment of mathematics in the text.

The problem of mathematical understanding that Feynman emphasizes should be eased by the advent of the computer in the classroom. Professor John Kemeny, the former president of Dartmouth College, and others have written enthusiastically of the potential role of the computer as a powerful new tool for teaching in general and, in particular, for helping students begin to understand sooner and better a variety of basic concepts. While eventually great gains can be realized through computer-based instruction, I have no illusions that they can be accomplished overnight.

The measure of the coming impact of computer technology on higher education will arise from the multitude of experiments now being conducted, or about to be tried, in universities across the land. One such endeavor, Project Athena, is a large-scale five-year experiment just beginning at M.I.T., which will integrate computers with advanced computational and graphics capabilities into undergraduate education throughout the institution. With the independent collaboration and active support of Digital Equipment Corporation and IBM, the experiment will involve the creation of extensive, coherent networks of computers with thousands of terminals that will enable individuals to share each other's information and programs and to work together on problems and ideas in new ways.

The whole of the Project Athena experiment is aimed at exploring most broadly the possibilities of producing significant changes in the teaching and learning of subjects in many different ways. It *is* an experiment, one based on the belief that personal computers and computer graphics can help students learn in new ways, even though no one knows *a priori* exactly how. The evolving exploitation of computer technology for educational purposes can only benefit from the great number and diversity of trials currently planned or underway, including those that fail as well as those that succeed.

Computers, however, will not provide, as best I can judge, the answer, the master key to free us from our problems in creating the substance of a modern liberal education. As suggested earlier, I do not believe there is some single and therefore "simple" solution, if only we could find it, to providing that substance. On the contrary, I am struck by the fact that those who are most persuaded of the urgent importance of such goals are unable to agree among themselves about just *how* to achieve them, not about how best to achieve them, but how to achieve them at all.

In bolstering the place of science in a liberal education, Feynman, for example, would stress mathematics; Kemeny and others, the use of computers instead; Fretter and I, a descriptive approach, building upwards from basic laws and basic building blocks; others would stress an historical approach; still others, relevance to everyday objects, gadgets or machines. The chemistry of cooking; the physics of music, of automobiles, of weather; the environment, ecology, energy waves—all have been suggested, and so have hands-on laboratory courses and hands-off lecture courses, films, demonstrations, descriptions of the universe—both now and then—

and careful analyses of a single experiment or of a single narrow field. No one of us, I must conclude, has the answer, but I also conclude that we must continue to seek—each of us in his own way—after the idea and the ideal of a liberal education.

The ideal of a liberal education must also include the idea that anyone who aspires to be educated in today's world must be thoroughly familiar with, must understand, other countries and other cultures. International understanding is not simply an educational ideal. In this nuclear age, when the consequences of our xenophobia could be irreversibly catastrophic, it is a prerequisite for survival. If education is going to do its part, the peculiarly American assumption that the whole world speaks—or ought to speak— our language, literally and metaphorically, must be left behind. We must begin by giving our students the skill in foreign languages that is indispensable to any effort to learn about other cultures. This means that training in language should begin with our early schooling and then continue throughout our education. Only then will we be able, as a society, to provide the kind of liberal learning that will permit us to understand our own diversity, to comprehend fully the endless variations on the theme of being human. The bitter experiences of this century, and the destructive power nuclear energy has given us, have lent this enterprise a new urgency. One great lesson of our time is the continuing triumph of tribalism over ideology; it is the lesson reported daily by the press from every corner of the world. It is a lesson that must be learned well and soon.

Here in the United States, suspicious as we may be of other nations, we have managed to break down the barriers of strangeness amongst ourselves and, with the profound exception of race, have come to know each other. We have achieved the uncommon feat of creating one people out of many. We have done it, overwhelmingly, through our system of education, which has given us the opportunity and the means to achieve a broader and more inclusive sense of identity.

The university has an especially important role to play as we seek to further our progress and extend our gains. While it has long been our goal that access to education, up to the highest levels, should be open to all on the basis of ability and talent alone, we have fallen far short of its attainment. The simple fact is that to be poor, to be a woman, or to be a member of a racial minority, has often blocked the way to the university, or at best has made access more difficult. Our aim must be to press constantly for change and progress, by acting affirmatively and vigorously until our educational institutions, including our universities, reasonably and responsibly reflect in their composition the demographics of the larger society. The data, which show that by 1990 a third of the eighteen-year-olds in the United States will be members of a minority group, require it; as do the ideals of our country and the needs of the world. Higher education alone cannot solve the problem of equal opportunity and access, but it has its proper, relevant and indispensable role, which it must play with determined purpose.

Our nation's universities and colleges must also recognize the developing career expectations and role of women—with the likely consequences for education at all levels, for the family, and society as a whole. As we look ahead at the changing lives of women and men, the data are startling and compelling. More than half of all current college students are women. Presently, moreover, well over half of newly hired workers in the United States are female. We can expect this proportion to be maintained for some years and to have its impact on the composition of the university and its employees, including the faculty. As we consider these engines for change in gender roles, it is clear that they are self-reinforcing and create one of the great social forces of our time. We have much to gain—all of us—from this evolution; but the gains will not come without stress, and we must be skillful, as well as willing, in adapting to them.

Do I have any illusions that these ideals—the ideal of scientific literacy; of a liberal education; of a just society; of the end of xenophobia; of, perhaps, the perfect university—can be achieved quickly? Of course not. Can they be achieved at all? I do not know. Is it purely visionary then to pursue them? Perhaps, but they must be pursued even so. Andrei Sakharov, the Soviet dissident who has written so well and so urgently about the threat of nuclear holocaust, put it this way: ". . . there is a need to create ideals even when you can't see any route by which to achieve them, because if there are no ideals then there can be no hope and then one would be completely in the dark. . . ."[4]

NOTES

1. Vannevar Bush, *Science—The Endless Frontier: A Report to the President on a Program for Postwar Scientific Research* (Washington, D.C.: U.S. Government Printing Office, 1945; New York: Arno Press, 1980).

2. Richard Feynman, *The Character of Physical Law* (Cambridge, Massachusetts: MIT Press, 1967), pp. 36, 39, 58.

3. William Fretter and David Saxon, *Physics for the Liberal Arts Student* (New York: Houghton Mifflin Co., 1971).

4. Andrei Sakharov, *Sakharov Speaks* (New York: Alfred A. Knopf, 1974), p. 173.

John B. Slaughter

University Research: Prospects and Problems

What are the prospects and problems facing university research today? In addressing this question, I first want to emphasize my optimistic belief that universities will continue to have the major responsibility for conducting basic research and for training researchers, despite many of the problems we face. While we must be diligent in making the public aware of both our contributions and our needs, we can expect a continuing commitment from the federal government—the major source of funding—to research and development. At the same time, universities across the nation are also benefitting from expanding partnerships with industry. Despite my general optimism about university research, I want to take this occasion to look at some of the problems—and possible solutions to them—that current economic realities present.

Federal Funding for Research and Development

The American public has come to recognize that research eventually returns a profit to society—an argument put forth by scientists in the fifties and sixties and confirmed by economists in the seventies. Today that relationship is evident in the continuing federal support for scientific research even in a time of economic crisis.

In a recent public opinion survey conducted for the National Science Foundation, 86 percent of the adults surveyed believe scientific discoveries are largely responsible for our standard of living in the United States, and 81 percent believe new discoveries will make our lives healthier, easier, and more comfortable. Technological know-how leads the list of eight factors judged to contribute most to America's influence in the world. It ranks ahead of our form of government, our economic system, our natural resources, our religious heritage, our educational system, and the racial and ethnic mixture of our population.

Public confidence in science and technology and the general awareness of the importance of research to the economy are being translated into public support for research and development. Federal funding for basic research in fiscal year 1983 was $5.9 billion. This amount is one percent above President Reagan's budget request and 9.9 percent above the fiscal year 1982 budget. In fiscal year 1984 we see an equally healthy 10 percent increase over fiscal year 1983 to $6.6 billion. Total research and development funding increased 18.2 percent between fiscal year 1983 and fiscal year 1984, from $40.4 billion to $47.8 billion. Given the fact that research has received more than its share of congressional sniping and administrative budget-cutting over the years, these figures have to be taken as a positive trend.

We must keep in mind, however, that federal support for research and development has just recently begun to shift toward defense and away from civilian areas, particularly health. Furthermore, support for basic research is growing at a slower rate than research and development funding generally. Large spending increases will not be targeted for basic research projects in the foreseeable future no matter how wise some of us believe such an investment to be.

Federal funding for university research and development is growing more slowly in part because of a greater emphasis on industry-conducted defense research. While universities will probably benefit from proposed increases in nondefense basic research in the physical sciences, mathematics, and engineering, the increases in this area are modest (9.9 percent between fiscal years 1983 and 1984) when compared to the large increase (27.9 percent) proposed for defense research and development. Universities will also have to absorb cutbacks in applied research in nondefense areas. An additional problem is that the defense-related areas of basic research targeted for major budget increases are precisely those in which universities are suffering the greatest faculty shortages.

A recent National Science Foundation report predicts that universities will increase their spending on research and development by about two percent a year through 1990, half the rate of the increases between 1975 and 1979. Federal support is expected to increase one percent a year compared with a three-percent annual increase in earlier periods, while nonfederal support will keep steady at a three-percent growth rate. A study by the Batelle Memorial Institute is slightly more optimistic, projecting a growth rate of four percent in research and development at universities in 1983. This projection is based on increases in private as well as public funding.

Industry Funding

Many research universities are making successful efforts to fund more of their own research and development with industry support. The fourteenth Report of the National Science Board, an historical review and analysis of industry-university interactions, states that at least half of four hundred companies queried value their university connection because it gives them "a window on new science and technology."[1] But the payoffs to industry of supporting universities encompass more than new knowledge. Equally important to the private sector is the development of trained manpower. When there is collaboration between university and industrial researchers on a project, with perhaps several industries participating, a dynamic knowledge-sharing takes place. The transfer of people from universities to industry, moreover, facilitates the transfer of knowledge.

While some industries are developing their own training programs, most manpower development will continue to occur in our nation's universities, and industry is beginning to recognize the importance of investing in that training. The University of Maryland, for example, recently received a major grant from the Westinghouse Corporation for the colleges of engineering, business, and management. For Westinghouse this support represents an investment in future manpower as well as an opportunity to support innovative research.

Problems Universities Face

Industry-university partnerships obviously will have a major impact on funding for university research and development in the future. However, these ties create problems that we are just beginning to confront.

Universities have a vested interest in academic freedom and the open exchange of ideas. Such an atmosphere is absolutely necessary for creative and productive research. At the same time, industry is legitimately concerned about protecting its rights to the results of the research it supports. Further, all participants in cooperative ventures need to know who has the right to publish results and who gets the patent rights and the royalties from the application in consumer products.

It is clear that we are a long way from a satisfactory resolution of these problems. Neither universities nor corporations are enthusiastic about national guidelines, but both sides see the need for consistency. Major research universities are drawing up their own guidelines, and some states are establishing "middleman" mechanisms, such as the North Carolina Biotechnology Foundation, to handle industrial contributions to university research.

Another problem that is no less significant is the orientation of industry-university partnerships toward short-term results having immediate applications. It is true that application in many fields is moving closer and closer to fundamental, basic research. We used to talk about an average of two decades between scientific discovery and its application in the marketplace; recently, especially in microelectronics and genetic engineering, that time span has been compressed into as little as two years. Nevertheless, we have to recognize that possible applications of most basic research are not apparent from the outset. Yet there is no question about the ultimate importance of creative research. Let me cite just one example. After twenty years of research on fruit flies, bacteriophages, and cell cultures in hundreds of university labs, molecular biology is "suddenly" blossoming into a new industry. We now anticipate profound benefits not just in new medical diagnoses and drugs, but in improved food crops as well. But none of these uses could have been developed without a long-standing and continuing effort simply to understand biological phenomena. Universities must guard against the temptation to shift support from basic research for what might seem to be more profitable short-term ventures.

At the same time, universities face an important dilemma in making long-term research commitments on the basis of federal funding. In the past thirty-five years, the federal government has become the primary source of all basic research support. Federal funding, however, has not been immune to political trends, and it is often difficult to predict the upcoming cycles in funding. Right now, for example, environmental research is "out," not because the national need in this area has abated, but because of a political decision to spend our money elsewhere. We need better long-range planning at the national level for scientific research and better coordination among the many agencies of the federal government that provide support for scientific research. The scientific community has a responsibility to monitor federal funding trends and to decide whether these trends serve the best interests of the nation.

Whether universities are involved in publicly or privately funded research, they face the problem of having to work with outdated and inadequate equipment and instrumentation. Equipment has become a very expensive, but very essential part of research, and many research universities lack the resources to make major investments in this area. Although many government agencies have established matching funds to help universities update their equipment, public universities in particular are hard pressed to find matching funds in amounts large enough to meet the cost of expensive equipment.

When universities do, in fact, generate some funds for the purchase of equipment, many public institutions find themselves faced with complicated and slow-moving state purchasing procedures. In Maryland it can take over nine months to process the papers for a small computer! Clearly, this is an area in which many state universities are demanding greater fiscal autonomy. Another serious problem is that once equipment is purchased, often in conjunction with a major building project, academic units within the university often lack the necessary funds to maintain it.

Universities and the Problem of Human Resources

Universities are in a unique position in the scientific research community. Not only do they bear a major responsibility for research, but they are also the principal sources of scientists and technologists who carry out the nation's research. Current faculty shortages in key scientific fields are handicapping us in the training of skilled manpower.

There are faculty shortages in university engineering and computer departments and in some medical schools. There are as many as 2,000 unfilled faculty positions in engineering in the nation's universities—a vacancy rate of ten percent. Likewise, there are approximately 200 vacancies in departments that specialize in the computer sciences. These vacancies are straining the instructional capacity of those schools and departments faced with insufficient personnel. The shortages of faculty are the result of declining numbers of doctorates and the availability of more attractive employment opportunities in industry for those who do have advanced degrees.

Federal Support for Graduate Education

In the mid-1960s the federal government awarded in one year 51,000 predoctoral fellowships across the entire range of academic disciplines, but principally in the physical and biomedical sciences. Each one of these fellowships brought with it funds for the cost of education, enabling the universities to waive tuition and to have funds in hand to purchase equipment, enlarge facilities, and create new tenured faculty positions in the science departments. We now have less than twenty percent of the number of awards given in 1966, and these are restricted to relatively few areas of study. Today we are able to count only 1,500 predoctoral fellowships awarded to students in the sciences and engineering.

These negative trends are being offset to some degree by certain positive developments, which reflect the concern of research leaders in federal agencies for maintaining a sound basic research program at the nation's universities and colleges. For instance, the Department of Defense has proposed expanding its graduate fellowship program. Awards for graduate study would be sufficiently generous to dissuade young men and women from embarking on careers in industry and business immediately after earning a bachelor's degree and to encourage them, instead, to invest in both themselves and the country. Similarly, the National Science Foundation is making moves to strengthen its own graduate fellowship program. Universities must encourage these trends by lobbying vigorously for more comprehensive and consistent government investment in training scientific researchers.

Precollege Math and Science Education

In addition to funding cutbacks and their ramifications, universities have to deal with the consequences of serious inadequacies in precollege science and mathematics education. Over the past few decades, scientific research in this nation has yielded extraordinary results. Paradoxically, in the last ten to fifteen years, we have

failed to nurture a key component necessary for the future of research activity—our primary and secondary schools. Scientific
research cannot exist without the educational system to foster it.
Currently we face a disturbing reality within our society in the
area of scientific education. We have for the most part developed a
broadly based educational system, but one which in recent years
has neglected the science and math education of large segments of
the population.

Gerald Holton, the distinguished historian of science, stated
the problem succinctly when he delivered the tenth annual Jefferson Lecture, sponsored by the National Endowment for the Humanities. "We are separating out into a knowledgeable scientific technological elite," he said, "and a large, uninformed, comfortable,
scientifically illiterate majority of people who have to throw themselves into the hands of the elite—or who, if they want to rebel,
must do it in uninformed ways, or just on intuition." The general
scientific illiteracy of our society presents a frightening prospect
for the future—a future that depends so heavily on scientific and
technological developments.

The problem of general scientific illiteracy is compounded by
the inadequate supply of science and mathematics teachers available right now. We have made education a decidedly unattractive
option for most scientists and mathematicians, who find better
pay and higher status in careers outside the classroom. Although
there are shortages generally in the science and technology workforce, the shortage of science and mathematics teachers is the most
severe. Nationwide, the annual vacancy rate for mathematics
teachers in the secondary schools is ten percent or higher. The
situation in the physical sciences is equally bad. When a school
district the size of Chicago can provide only one qualified high
school physics teacher for every two high schools, imagine what
the situation must be in Peoria and Kankakee.

Colleges and universities, particularly research universities,
have been derelict in not taking more responsibility for the preparation of new and better-qualified teachers. The trite and tired
responses of most colleges of education are part of the problem.

Finally, I do not believe that excellence and equality in education are mutually exclusive. More than ever, universities have a responsibility to develop an educational system that ensures access to scientific professions for groups that are currently underrepresented. Despite the progress made in the past decade, women and minorities continue to be underrepresented in the science and engineering fields. We cannot continue to waste such potentially valuable resources if we want to expand our capacities for creative research.

Conclusion: Future Prospects

Although I have outlined some of the problems facing universities and the nation, I believe universities will continue to occupy a central place in the research establishment. They can look forward to greater industry support and continued government funding. Moreover, the government is developing new ways to foster industry-university cooperation. The tax incentives for industry included in the Economic Recovery Act of 1981, which make support of research a little easier and allow deductions for donating scientific equipment to universities, are one example. The National Science Foundation's support for Industry/University Cooperative Research Projects is another.

Given the many constraints under which universities operate, I think the vitality of scientific research on campuses across the nation is remarkable. The public has a vested interest in nurturing creativity and dedication. In our pursuit of excellence in science and education, we are, in fact, engaged in what H. G. Wells has labeled "a race between education and catastrophe."[2] We cannot afford to repeat the failures of the past decade. We must find innovative, consistent ways to improve the quality of education, and we must find the funds to support those efforts.

Margaret Mead once said that "we are now at the point where we must educate people in what nobody knew yesterday, and prepare in our schools for what no one knows yet but what some people must know tomorrow." We must ensure equal access to the opportunities that such knowledge opens. We must encourage public support for scientific research, and we must translate that support into adequate and consistent funding for creative research— funding that does not fluctuate with changes in the political and economic climate. To do less would be to deprive future generations of the political and economic security they deserve to enjoy.

NOTES

1. *University-Industry Research Relationships: Myths, Realities, and Potential*, 14th Annual Report of the National Science Board to the President and the Congress (Washington, D.C.: National Science Foundation, 1982).

2. H. G. Wells, *The Outline of History* (Garden City, New York: Doubleday, 1971).

Howard E. Simmons, Jr., and Alan McClelland

Private Industry and University Research

Until the nineteenth century, perhaps the mid-nineteenth century, research conducted at universities and colleges was regarded as isolated from everyday activity—i.e., the "ivory tower" concept. Many thought of universities as a special kind of sanctuary in which scholars pursued their studies undisturbed by the intrusions of mundane affairs. By the last quarter of the last century, however, as the fruits of organized experimentation by the Edisons, Bells, and Marconis appeared, the practical value of organized research in science and technology became evident to all. Great interest in what was going on in the ivory tower was generated by the technical inventions and discoveries of the era. Industry and government began a major involvement in technological research, and the triumverate nature of the United States research enterprise—universities, government, and industry—was established. Ever since, university research has been an integral part of a larger enterprise, not an isolated activity.

Though the industrial research establishment, the junior partner in the American research enterprise, is now larger than its senior academic counterpart, industry's recognition of the crucial importance of university research is stronger than ever. The continued growth in the twentieth century of research and development as a separate, definable activity has, if anything, strengthened the realization of mutual dependency of the three main partners— academia, government, and industry. As with the legs of a three-legged stool, there can be no real difference in importance. Instead, the important questions relate to defining the role of each partner.

Industry, with seventy-four percent of the nation's scientists and engineers engaged in research and development (on a full-time equivalent basis) and annually performing $65 billion worth, clearly has a huge stake in how research and development activities are organized and distributed through our society.[1] Yet never has there been a clearer recognition by industry of the importance of university research and, in particular, of its contribution to the success of industrial research and development efforts.

Because the university portion of the nation's research and development activity is not carried out in isolation, it is most meaningful to discuss university research in terms of its relationships to the other two players in the drama. From the industrial side, it is most appropriate to discuss industry-university relationships, particularly since most research interactions tend primarily to involve two of the partners, rather than all three simultaneously.

In attempting to summarize industrial perspectives on industry-university research interactions, three key points stand out:

1) Academic-industrial research interactions are neither new nor of only transitory importance. Thus, attention should be centered on defining those patterns of interaction which will be useful for many years to come, with a careful view backward to assess the successes and failures of the past for guidance in negotiating a future course.

2) The institutions in each segment of the research triad must accurately understand their own roles and ensure that research interactions with others promote, rather than detract from, those roles. There is a real value to some overlap of roles—overlap can greatly enhance effective interaction by increasing mutual understanding—but major

deviation from proper roles by any of the three types of institutions can produce results ranging from ineffective at best to damaging at worst.

3) Many different types of interactions can be effective. Because "university research" can properly include everything from very esoteric theoretical research to highly specific applied development, appropriate industry-university interactions can cover an equally wide range of possibilities. Each interaction should be viewed on its own merits; there is no way to define a single "right" form of interaction. However, each institution must also keep track of the sum total of all its interactions to ensure a sound balance.

To contribute some perspective, a look backward in support of the first point is a good start. Recent rhetoric often seems to regard industry-university research interactions as a brand new concept— a unique invention of our times. In fact, the research establishments of the universities and industry have been very closely involved in many areas for years. It does seem true, however, that never has there been a time when it was a more important or visible subject. As Dr. Lewis M. Branscomb, chairman of the National Science Board, wrote not long ago, ". . . 1980 and 1981 turned out to be boom years for relationships between campuses and corporations. . . . these enhanced activities have persisted despite economic difficulties in 1981 and 1982."[2] If anything, they are continuing to expand today.

The 1930 Annual Report of the Central Chemical Department of the DuPont Company, the predecessor of the company's present Central Research and Development Department, emphasizes the importance attached to industry-university research relationships even a half-century ago:

It has been evident during the past year, as a result of following closely the foreign developments, particularly, that our fundamental research has become of increasing importance. In the past, the scientific work of universities was free for exploitation by industry, but it now appears that any new scientific developments in pure research work that have the prospect of any commercial utilization are brought to the attention of certain companies, and patents are taken out before the results are released in publications. We have noticed that some of the most important chemical developments carried out recently in German universities were assigned to the I.G. We also know that, even in this country, many of the men engaged in scientific work in our universities are now attached to companies as consultants, and the results of their work are covered by patents assigned to the companies by which they are employed, if there is any prospect of use. There has never been a time when competition is so keen in research as it is today. Every field of chemistry is being searched for new ideas that can be harnessed to practical applications. The industry must rely more than ever upon its own efforts for new methods and products for which new uses can be found. Fundamental research, therefore, occupies an increasingly important place in our research program.[3]

It is evident that Dr. C. M. A. Stine, director and author of the report for the Central Chemical Department, clearly understood a number of things equally true today: 1) fundamental research is the base upon which applications must be built; 2) university or faculty agreements with industry can have significant consequences on dissemination of university research discoveries; and 3) there is a place for fundamental research in industry. Thus, four years earlier, in 1926, Dr. Stine had initiated a program of fundamental research in the department ". . . without thought of profit through the medium of practical applications . . . . " though he also added, "If the volume is sufficiently great . . . wisely directed . . . well done, I believe practical applications are certain to result." Moreover, it is interesting to note that another serious danger is stated in Stine's 1926 memo outlining the beginning of the DuPont Company's fundamental research program:

[It was] recently emphasized by Mr. Herbert C. Hoover, that, as measured by expenditures, the volume of fundamental work is rapidly losing ground as compared with the volume of applied research. In other words, applied research is facing a shortage of its principal raw materials.[4]

Obviously, we in the 1980s are not the first to recognize this danger.

While the above examples demonstrate that today's concerns are not new, current conditions have added an urgency to their consideration. The recent phenomenal progress in biological research and its potential implications for practical applications in medicine and agriculture are generating much concern on how best to translate these discoveries into useful products. The vastly greater role of the federal government in research funding now than in Dr. Stine's day escalates the importance of relationships between that branch of the research community and both industry and the universities. The great increase in the proportion of our nation's population obtaining college degrees, including graduate degrees, also affects the picture, since most academic research is actually carried out by graduate and postdoctoral students. Thus, while there have been substantial industry-university interactions for many years, each era, including this one, does bring its own particular conditions. The challenge is to develop mutually beneficial research interactions that meet current needs yet do not in the long run work to the detriment of any segment of the nation's total research structure.

Industry and Government Research Roles

A clear recognition of the purpose of research activities in each of the three segments of the national research community is basic to any discussion of how the segments should interrelate. Industry has perhaps the most unilateral approach; almost all industrial research and development has product development as its ultimate goal. While that goal can encompass some research which is only indirectly related to a product, the role of industry as a whole in our society rather clearly assigns product development to industrial research and development as the primary mission. In general, industry has been quite successful in meeting its research objective of innovation—the term that refers to the total process of development and commercialization of new products and business services. Innovation by its nature is a risky and uncertain activity, and therefore many attempted developments have failed. But the successes far outweigh the failures, and, in fact, businesses with the poorest performance generally have been those which failed to try to innovate rather than those which have been unsuccessful in some of their attempts.

The role of government (primarily at the federal level) in research is a dual one: to do research, but more importantly to provide extensive funding for research in both industry and the universities. Government supported industry research—thirty-three percent of industrial research is funded by government—is predominantly for the development of products, mostly military, which the government, as a customer, needs.[5] Conversely, most government supported university research is of a more fundamental nature.

Though government research is not a primary topic in this analysis, a slight digression may help to prove our point about the importance of understanding and respecting the proper roles of the three partners in the United States research establishment. The record of government in undertaking commercial developments—in all countries—is overwhelmingly bad. Nelson and Langlois in *Science* offer the following conclusion about government research involvement in commercial ventures: "Here the historical record seems, for a change, unequivocal. Unequivocally negative." The kind of government involvement in research funding to which they refer is typified by the Air Force's SST and by Operation Breakthrough of the Department of Housing and Urban Affairs. They explain that "In both cases, . . . the federal agencies attempted to insert themselves into the business of developing particular technologies for a commercial market in which they had little or no procurement interest," and conclude that the resulting problem was not a "specific" one of failing to hire necessary expertise, but rather: "The lesson is a general one, about the location of knowledge and the mechanism of its transmission in the R & D system."[6] Other examples of similarly misguided government research efforts are the joint British-French Concorde aircraft and Telematique, "a grand, multibillion-dollar program to develop information processing gear [for] every French household," which is "still on square one" five years after the plan was initiated.[7] The primary reason for such failures is government trying to operate outside its role— trying to carry out a commercial innovation function it is neither designed nor equipped to perform.

University Research Roles

Research in the university, our primary topic here, is more complex, or multifaceted, than in either of the other two segments. It serves one or more of the following functions, which are not mutually exclusive:

1) *Advance knowledge.* Research for this purpose is the sort generally referred to as "fundamental" or "basic." While a significant amount of basic work is done in both industry and government, the great bulk of such research is conducted in the academic world. Because the university world is so effective and so dominant in this area, it is extremely important that university research to advance basic knowledge be kept healthy. In the long run, industry is highly dependent on the underpinning of fundamental research for its applied work, though the chronology may vary from project to project. Sometimes theory leads and application follows. Conversely, theory may follow to explain an empirically discovered application. This is even more true today than when Dr. Stine and President Hoover noted as much over fifty years ago.

2) *Educate students.* While the knowledge developed through research is "science," the conduct of research is an art. Like all arts, it is usually best learned by doing, and by doing at the feet of a master. A student does not become a skilled researcher while sitting in lectures; that skill is acquired in the laboratory or in the field. Although the student produces results—new knowledge—while learning to do research, the development of the student's skills may be much more important than the knowledge. Although this educative research function falls almost exclusively within the university's domain, it is of crucial importance to the entire research establishment.

3) *Serve the public.* A substantial amount of university research is directed more to serving a perceived public need than to advancing basic knowledge, though this role often is overlooked. Agricultural research presents many examples; much of it is highly applied research specifically intended to benefit farmers. That farmers constitute a "public" is a consensus developed seventy-five to one hundred years ago and expressed, for example, through legislation such as the Morrill Act of 1862, which established the land-grant college system to promote the "agricultural and mechanical arts." The service role played by academic agricultural research certainly deserves a large share of the credit for the preeminence of American agriculture, a commendable achievement that has served the nation well. Service-directed research can be a valid and important component of the university research spectrum, but it can also become ineffectual by extending into areas more suited to industrial research. Thus, implementation of the service-research function requires a clear understanding and justification of that role for any given program, i.e., a careful determination that the provision of the service in question is appropriate to the aims and character of academic research.

Industry-University Interactions

Interaction of private industry with university research can be structured in many different ways to take into account the particular interests and objectives of the participants. In setting up the arrangement for such interactions, it is important first to reach a clear and mutual understanding about how a particular university research program fits within the three research roles of knowledge advancement, education, and service. Second, agreement must be reached on procedures best suited to the operational patterns that are basic to the academic world. One fundamental element of those organizational patterns was cited by John McArthur, dean of the Harvard Business School: "Academia is a world of solo performers. Almost all serious work is done on an individual basis."[8] As applied to the laboratory-based disciplines, this does not mean that the professor lacks the support of the usual group of graduate and postdoctoral students. But it does mean that normally each faculty member has his or her own separate research program. While cooperation with other faculty members is not uncommon, the basic independence of each is very deeply ingrained. In contrast, the industrial research world requires a much higher degree of organization and teamwork to carry out its basic mission of industrial innovation. Innovation usually involves a far more hierarchical structure than that which operates in the university research environment. Dr. Edward E. David, Jr., president of Exxon Research and Engineering Company and former science adviser to President Nixon, highlights this characteristic:

> Our engineering people become involved at a very early stage with research. The coupling of research and engineering here is very, very high because it enables us in an early stage of research to direct it in such a way that it will produce an economic development in the long run. It also keeps the research from going off in oblique directions. And yet you leave enough leeway in the process that new things can be done and researchers can follow some of their hints and ideas.[9]

The fact that very different structural patterns exist in business and educational institutions is as it should be because their roles in the research enterprise are different. Failure to recognize the differences or to accept each partner as having its proper place can be a major source of breakdown of industry-university interactions. In contrast to the approach Dr. David describes, academic science researchers seldom see the involvement of either industrial or academic engineering personnel as appropriate even after a substantial amount of time, to say nothing of early involvement. Instead, the usual channel for moving university *science* research into an industrial development chain is through industrial *scientists,* who in due course interact with their own engineering people. The concept of some overlapping of academic and industrial research activities is crucially important here. People in different organizations doing most nearly the same type of work will interact most effectively, i.e., university scientists are likely to work best with industrial scientists involved in the long-range end of industrial research, and university people involved in product applications (about which more will be said later) are apt to cooperate most effectively with product development people in industry. If industry-university interactions do not follow this principle, they will be mutually frustrating at the least; more likely, they will quickly fall apart.

Overlap can be important to successful industry-university collaboration in another respect as well. Companies heavily involved in doing research, particularly if they perform some long-range or fundamental research, can most clearly appreciate the complementary nature of academic and industrial research efforts. This observation is supported by the National Science Board, which noted that "The companies that developed major in-house research laboratories have been the strongest supporters of academic research."[10] In this general context, people transfers are of potential significance as a type of interaction that promotes mutual understanding concerning the differences in university and industry research perspectives and at the same time enhances recognition of their complementarity and interdependence. While often overlooked in the course of the inevitable concentration on money as the prime lubricant of interaction, the temporary movement of mature researchers across the academic-industrial boundary—in both directions—offers excellent research opportunities. Experience in the Central Research and Development Department of DuPont, for example, has been quite positive in regard to such arrangements. Academic scientists have spent periods ranging from a few weeks to two years in DuPont facilities in mutually beneficial research projects. Conversely, many DuPont scientists have joined university laboratories on the same kind of temporary research stay. These interchanges of people have occurred not only in conjunction with American universities, but with foreign institutions as well; and this international aspect has also proved to be highly beneficial.

Differences in industry and university research roles and organizational structure as they affect the dissemination of research results is another area with great potential for frustration and misunderstanding. Industry, whose interest in patent protection and in gaining competitive advantage is normally strong, has a natural tendency to want to keep research findings confidential if the results are seen as possibly important. The academic world, in contrast, has dissemination of knowledge as its fundamental purpose for existence. In all three university research functions— advancement of knowledge, student education, and public service—distribution of the results of research outside the institution is an inextricable component. The inherent connection between dissemination and advancement of knowledge is so obvious as to need no comment. In educating students in the art of research, the presentation of research results, both orally and in writing, is one of the crucial skills students must learn. While this could be done within a limited group inside or outside the university, interaction with the whole professional community is such an integral part of the art of conducting research that depriving the student of this opportunity would seriously compromise the quality of graduate education.

The public service function is more complex in respect to dissemination of knowledge, requiring careful consideration of who the "public" is in each case. The more extensive the restrictions placed on dissemination of information, however, the more questionable is the classification "public service." Industry, therefore, must recognize that only very minimal restrictions on the dissemination of research results are proper, and the university must insist on the freedom to carry out the inherent communication roles of the institution. Rockefeller University, for example, in formulating institutional policies for industrial sponsorship of research, has addressed the issue of university responsibility for the transmission of knowledge:

> Basic principles: The University's primary mission is to carry out fundamental scientific investigations *pro bono humani generis*, for the good of mankind.
>
> Any Agreement for industrial sponsorship of research on campus will emphasize the University's basic mission and the traditions related to it. It will give the principal investigator(s) full responsibility for, and broad flexibility in, the direction of work—stringently minimizing the amount and degree of any proprietary or confidential information associated with the work in order to foster the traditionally open pattern of creative interactions among other laboratories at the University and with the scientific community generally.
>
> The Principal Investigator and colleagues will possess the full traditional freedom to publish and present promptly all results of research. Only minimal delays (typically 30 days) will be accommodated for consideration of filing patent applications prior to scientific communication.[11]

The issues surrounding patentability of industry sponsored university research and the potential value of such patents represent still another area in which misunderstandings on both sides frequently arise. Patents are certainly important, and the possibility of patentable results should not be overlooked. There is no area, however, in which the imagination as easily gets out of hand. Some numbers may help put things in perspective. Dr. Edmond D'Ouville, director of Technical Liaison, Patents and Licensing

Department, Standard Oil (Indiana), has reported the following results on his organization's patent experience:

> From 1956 through 1965 we considered 7,460 invention disclosures submitted by employees, primarily the company's R & D staff. During those ten years, 1770 patent applications were filed; thus one out of four disclosures resulted in an application. During the same decade, 1384 U.S. patents were obtained.
>
> Five years later, in 1970, we tried to evaluate these patents in terms of monetary value to the company. This was a difficult assignment, even having the advantage of hindsight. I know it would have been much more difficult had we tried to do it any earlier.
>
> One observation is that more than 90 percent of the patents were granted to only 5 percent of the R & D staff. The motivation was presumably the same for all. The profilic inventors apparently had either more inventive skills, better opportunities, or both. Other companies have observed similar results.
>
> Another observation was that in terms of value to the company five of the patents proved to be worth more than all the others. Three were gold mines in the million-dollar class, serving as the basis for new businesses and licensing. Many of course were of no apparent value, and two led to substantial losses when put into practice.[12]

These results from a large, experienced industrial research organization graphically demonstrate how low the probability is of any specific project turning out a really lucrative patent. Since the academic researcher, even on a project supported by industry, normally does not have a patent as the primary goal, the probability of a "gold mine in the million-dollar class" is presumably even smaller than in the situation cited above. This suggests that neither the academic nor the industrial partners should expect much in terms of highly valuable patents out of university research. If the industrial sponsor expects that the research is likely to lead to extremely important patents, it is probably making a mistake to sponsor the research in a university; the project should be done in-house for greater protection and control. If the university researcher is primarily seeking valuable patents, he or she is probably working in the wrong place. While some valuable patents have come out of the university world, and the possibility of more is always there, the great majority of important patents in this century have come from industry. Patents are a by-product of university research, not the primary product.

In establishing procedures for obtaining patents and negotiating licensing agreements under them, universities must balance the need for confidentiality, on the one side, and open communication of scientific results, on the other. The Rockefeller University policy statement quoted above is one example illustrating how universities engaged with industry might realize the financial value of research programs without inappropriate delay in dissemination of research results or undue involvement in product development. More importantly, however, carefully prepared guidelines for securing patents and licenses may actually serve the public good by providing the proprietary protection necessary to allow some industrial firm to convert the discovery to a commercial product. In some cases, a valuable discovery may never be turned into a useful product because no business is able to take the financial risk involved in developing an unprotectable product. Those who have not been involved in the "development" portion of "R&D" often fail to realize that most of the expense, and therefore most of the risk, comes after the research has proceeded a considerable distance. An inexact but still useful DuPont rule of thumb is that the development expenses will be at least twenty-fold greater than the cost of the research necessary to bring the new product to a reasonably complete definition.

Besides anticipating likely areas of conflict so as to prevent difficulties from developing in industry-university relationships, it is necessary also to determine where a proposed industry sponsored academic research project fits into the company's spectrum of research and development. This is an especially important point because there are various possible "fits," and they are not always what might be expected at first glance. Pharmaceutical research, for example, of necessity depends very heavily on clinical testing in medical schools or government hospitals and clinics. This is of course an absolutely critical stage of product development; the law permits no pharmaceutical to be sold before it is rigorously tested. Moreover, the product potential is normally unclear until the clinical stage has been completed. Therefore, in the pharmaceuticals product area, the academic world is inextricably bound up in the product development portion of the research and development spectrum to a far greater degree than in any other product line. This obviously puts a very different complexion on agreements for joint or sponsored research. Patents, confidentiality, liability, and other agreement elements assume a different character.

The pharmaceutical model also illustrates the "public service" component, with often a considerably smaller "fundamental" role. This is perhaps a point of view some will quarrel with, for the definition of fundamental research is a hazy one. Recognizing that the purpose of most clinical pharmaceutical testing is to define an effective treatment for a disease, the work inevitably has to focus on practical utility more than on contribution to fundamental understanding of the disease. Understanding of disease or resistance mechanisms and other scientific issues may ultimately result from subsequent research, but a pharmaceutical is intended to improve the condition of a patient and that must be the foremost objective in clinical testing. The ethics of clinical testing are demanding. The academic clinician testing new drugs is performing one of the most important kinds of public service; the advancement of scientific knowledge *per se* must take second place.

A second example, in which university research occupies an intermediate position in the research and development spectrum, is the agrichemical area. For years, many university agriculture departments and agricultural experiment stations have played a very crucial role in the development of scientific agriculture and the products that make it possible. Again, it is interesting to look at the balance of the "fundamental" and "service" components. Since the ethical complications of treating a corn plant with an experimental drug are vastly less restrictive than the drug/human analog, the two motives for research can be blended more easily to the researcher's own interests. This also means that the manufacturer of agrichemical products, in contrast to pharmaceutical products, is much less dependent on the university researcher; industrial firms can and do maintain very extensive field testing facilities. But agrichemical firms also provide extensive support to research in the universities because university people in many ways represent the agrichemical firms' customers, the farmers. Nelson and Langlois have dubbed this phenomenon "Clientele-oriented Applied R & D." They deem this a "strikingly successful government program of applied R & D" and ask, "what special conditions have made this applied R & D program feasible and productive?" Their conclusions about the agricultural industry (by which they specifically mean the farmers, not the companies that supply farmers) are as follows:

> . . . agricultural history . . . is largely atomistic in form . . . fellow competitors are seen as inherently less threatening in farming than in most industries; technological knowledge is therefore far less proprietary, and there is a public cast to the results of even very applied R & D . . . farmers see it as advantageous to them to advance even very specific technologies as quickly as possible.[13]

Here, then, is a case in which the academic world has a pattern of very effective service to an appreciative (and politically potent) clientele and has supported that applied "service" research in conjunction with a reasonable amount of more fundamental research. This "service" relation of the universities with the farmers provides industry with a way to get "closer to its customers" through rather extensive research support of university people in agriculture.

Agrichemical companies support a great deal of university research to test the effectiveness of their new products on crops important to the farmers in the region the university serves. This arrangement is useful to farmer and agrichemical manufacturer. Much of the research conducted by the university occurs very late in the product development cycle; the manufacturer has developed the product and its manufacturing process, tested it internally on its own test plots, and is finally ready to have the internal results publicly corroborated. University research thus serves both a technical function by providing further performance data on a variety of crops under a variety of conditions and a marketing function by establishing the product's credibility with local farmers.

Thomas J. Peters and Robert H. Waterman, Jr., in their book *In Search of Excellence: Lessons from America's Best-Run Companies,* formulate some sound principles, which can pull together a number of these ideas.[14] Peters and Waterman carefully selected a substantial sample of continuously innovative big companies—sixty-two in all—which met a strict set of performance standards over at least twenty years, then completed an in-depth analysis of these corporations to determine their definitive characteristics. On casual reading, their findings seem deceptively simple, but in fact are quite profound. Among the attributes that Peters and Waterman conclude characterize excellent, innovative companies, two are particularly germane in the present context: "close to the customer," and "stick to the knitting." These attributes are disarmingly simple, but crucially important. Expanding on "close to the customer," they say:

> These companies learn from the people they serve. . . . Many of the innovative companies get their best product ideas from customers. That comes from listening, intently and regularly.[15]

They also point out that economist Christopher Freeman, in a study of 39 innovations in the chemical industry and 33 in scientific instrumentation, found that only 15 of 200 proposed measures of innovation were statistically significant in predicting success or failure. The number-one factor was that "successful firms understand user needs better" than less successful firms do. Freeman concluded:

> Successful firms pay more attention to the market than do failures. Successful innovators innovate in response to market needs, involve potential users in the development of the innovation, and understand user needs better.[16]

"Stick to the knitting" is Peters and Waterman's shorthand for the finding that "While there were a few exceptions, the odds for excellent performance seem strongly to favor those companies that stay reasonably close to businesses they know." Elsewhere in the volume, they further elaborated:

> Our principal finding is clear and simple. Organizations that do branch out (whether by acquisition or internal diversification) but stick very close to their knitting out-perform the others . . . . Thus it would appear that some diversification is a basis for stability through adaption, but that willy-nilly diversification doesn't pay by any measure. . . virtually *every* academic study has concluded that unchanneled diversification is a losing proposition.[17]

What is the significance of these results for industry-university relationships? Product development is an inherent part of the research and development spectrum and, as we have seen, involves the university world as well as the industrial world. Therefore, it can be very instructive to participants on both sides of the academic-industrial fence to look carefully at how successful product innovation occurs. In developing research interactions, both parties need to determine whether the true objectives have been carefully thought through and whether the proposed pattern of interaction is wisely related to those objectives. For example, if the work under consideration is really quite product-oriented (e.g., defining or rediscovering a totally new product or testing a product already part way through the development process), the people and organizational units involved should meet both the "customer" and "knitting" criteria above. As previously cited, agriculture school researchers are often very "close to the customer," the farmer. Medical school clinicians, too, are very close to the ultimate customer, the patient, though in another sense they—physicians—are themselves really the customers. After all, use of prescription drugs is on the order of the doctor, not the patient. In other words, following the dictates of Peters and Waterman, these two groups in the university research community may be very effective contributors to product development, i.e., the later phases of the innovation process.

Conversely, university professors in the "pure" science departments often have absolutely no contact with "the customer," and, in fact, are quite vociferous about wanting none. This is reasonable; the principal research function of these departments is to carry out fundamental or basic research. And this purpose strongly dictates the type of interactions that will be most effective. In "pure" science departments, industry generally should support long-range research not oriented toward specific products—the very earliest part of the innovation process. The interactions are best handled through the company researchers who themselves are involved in the longest-range, most fundamental portions of the company's research program. Both sides should work very hard not to let "visions of sugarplums" go "dancing through their heads." Prior agreements should deal reasonably with the possibility of a discovery of direct commercial value, but should recognize that the probability is low. Writing advance agreements covering improbable events is always difficult—the imagination easily gets out of hand. There is even a good deal to be said—lawyers notwithstanding—for assuming that a mutually fair agreement can be reached *after* a discovery has been made and defined.

A few details of a well-known development from DuPont's past—neoprene—may help illustrate how fundamental university research can fit into innovation. DuPont had been seeking, unsuccessfully, for over four years to develop a synthetic rubber, when Dr. Elmer Bolton heard a paper in 1925 by Father Julius Nieuwland of the University of Notre Dame. This paper on his discovery of the synthesis of divinylacetylene from acetylene was given at the first organic symposium of the American Chemical Society. Recognizing it as possibly useful in DuPont's research on synthetic rubber, Dr. Bolton arranged a consulting agreement with Father Nieuwland, and later added provision for royalties to Notre Dame if any of his inventions were commercialized. Neoprene, chemically polychloroprene, was discovered by Wallace Carothers and Arnold Collins, both DuPont employees, while studying the purification of

divinylacetylene. They isolated chloroprene, the monomer for neoprene, discovered its polymerization to a useful material, and developed the commercial process for its manufacture. Because their
process used the catalyst discovered and used by Nieuwland in his
divinylacetylene synthesis, Notre Dame received $2 million in
royalties. Even though Nieuwland did not discover neoprene or the
process used to manufacture it, his fundamental work, combined
with the product-directed work of the DuPont chemists, led to a
new product of great significance. The crucial point here: the university science professor usually does not make the direct commercial discovery—nothing in his or her environment has been
designed to produce commercial discoveries. But doing what a
research science professor is skilled at doing—fundamental research—
in an environment ideally suited for that, may very well mesh
with industry's special skill—product and process development—in
a very useful way.

The current high level of positive and constructive attention to
the possibilities for cooperation of many sorts between the research
arms of the academic and industrial worlds is highly desirable and
deserves further cultivation.[18] If the parties involved will take
advantage of the lessons available from the long history of such
relationships, recognize the importance of full clarification of the
objectives of each party to such arrangements, and ensure that the
nature of each agreement truly fits the inherent characteristics of
the institutions and situations involved, the results can be very
beneficial. The research and development activities of academia,
government, and industry are highly interdependent; smooth
meshing of these activities serves all three segments, and thereby,
the nation as well. Just as in a smoothly functioning gear-train, the
gears must each rotate about their own axes, yet be far enough
apart to prevent binding, so must the three research partners be
positioned properly for the good of all.

NOTES

1. National Science Foundation, *Science and Technology Data Book* (Washington, D.C.: National Science Foundation, 1983), pp. 5, 7.

2. National Science Board, *University-Industry Research Relationships: Selected Studies,* Publication NSB 82-2 (Washington, D.C.: National Science Foundation, 1983), p. vii.

3. C. M. A. Stine, "Annual Report of the Central Chemical Department, 1930" (E. I. DuPont de Nemours Company, Wilmington, Delaware, 1930).

4. C. M. A. Stine, memo describing a program for initiating fundamental research in the Central Chemical Department, E. I. DuPont de Nemours Company, Wilmington, Delaware, 1926.

5. National Science Foundation, *Science Resources Studies: Highlights,* Publication NSF 83-314 (Washington, D.C.: National Science Foundation, 1984), pp. 2-3.

6. R. R. Nelson and R. N. Langlois, "Industrial Innovation Policy: Lessons from American History," *Science* 219 (1983), pp. 814-818. See, also, R. W. Schmitt, "National R & D Policy: An Industrial Perspective," *Science* 224 (1984), pp. 1806-1809.

7. "Telematique: A French Export That Doesn't Travel Well," *Business Week* (4 July 1983), p. 79.

8. J. E. McArthur, "Crisis in Higher Education . . . and Opportunities," *Chemtech* 13 (1983), pp. 338-9.

9. "Exxon's David Assesses Innovation," *Chemical & Engineering News* (5 December 1983), p. 10.

10. National Science Board, *University-Industry Research.*

11. Rockefeller University, "Outline of Policy: Themes to Be Covered in Major Agreements for Industrial Sponsorship of Research" (Rockefeller University, New York, May 1982, mimeographed).

12. Edmond D'Ouville, *Compensation for Employed Inventors* (Washington, D.C.: American Chemical Society Committee on Patent Matters and Related Legislation, March 1976), p. 7.

13. Nelson and Langlois, "Industrial Innovation Policy."

14. Thomas J. Peters and Robert H. Waterman, Jr., *In Search of Excellence: Lessons from America's Best-Run Companies* (New York: Harper and Row, 1982).

15. Ibid.

16. Cited in Peters and Waterman, *In Search of Excellence.*

17. Peters and Waterman, *In Search of Excellence.*

18. Recent publications reviewing various aspects of industry-university research relationships include the following: *Industrial-Academic Interfacing*, American Chemical Society, Symposium Series No. 244, 1984; *Partners in the Research Enterprise: University-Corporate Relations in Science and Technology*, University of Pennsylvania Press, 1983; *University-Industry Interaction: Guide to Developing Fundamental Research Agreements*, The Council For Chemical Research, Inc., P.O. Box AJ, Allentown, PA 18106. The last publication is a pamphlet that contains samples of legal agreements useful in industry-supported university fundamental research.

Richard L. Venezky

The Impact of Computer Technology on Higher Education

Predicting the impact of computer technology on higher education belongs properly to the art and science of prophecy, which is a field not generally taught at colleges and universities today. Nevertheless, prophecy strategies have been employed from biblical times to the present day, and two in particular merit consideration for our purposes here. The first, favored by politicians and others of like verbosity, is best represented by the ancient priestess of Apollo at Delphi and by the sixteenth-century French physician and astrologer, Nostradamus. The former spoke in riddles that even contemporary soothsayers found difficult to interpret, while the latter depended upon indirection, ambiguity, and a less than translatable mixture of languages to render even *post hoc* identification difficult. The second strategy, which is evidenced daily in the sports columns of many newspapers, combines simple probability with an astute evaluation of current information to predict, among other events, the point spreads in athletic contests. Although more science than art, the lack of extensive competition in this field attests to the severe difficulty of its mastery.

If I were totally uncertain of the impact of computer technology on higher education, I would adopt the former strategy and in effect say no more than did the comedian Mort Sahl when he declared, "The future lies ahead." And if I were dead certain of precisely what this impact would be, I would adopt the latter strategy and quote odds on the likelihood of different potential outcomes. But an objective analysis of technology, history, and education leaves me somewhat in between these poles, confident of certain outcomes but unwilling to risk hard-earned cash on many others. What I will do, therefore, is to peel back three layers of this issue, working from the more certain and observable outer skin to the inner and more hidden reaches. Whether the stripping of the final layer will reveal a coarse and pungent onion for higher education's future or a soft and delectable artichoke I will not reveal just now. In the interest of brevity, however, I will forego the customary pedantic definition of terminology, other than to qualify that computer technology includes not only computer hardware and software, but also data storage and transmission mechanisms and processes and the attendant sciences that have grown up around these advances over the last forty years.

The Outer Layer

The first prediction that can be made with high certainty about computer technology in higher education is that the incorporation of computers into nearly every facet of campus operations will continue and probably accelerate over the next decade. From control of heating and cooling to the library catalogue to student registration and campus publications, computer involvement will be the norm. In other words, to paraphrase Wordsworth, the use of computers will be as "continuous as the stars that shine and twinkle on the Milky Way." However, these will be gradual changes, which, judging from similar phenomena in industry and government, will not precipitate fundamental alterations in higher education's structures, goals, or general operating procedures.

Computer usage will also continue to increase in research, instruction, and administration, although the rate of increase and the distribution of new usages will probably be different from those of the past fifteen years. While today more than fifty percent of most university computing budgets are absorbed by administrative computing, future growth in this sector should be slower than in research and instruction.[1] Budgets for computing, figured as a percentage of the total expenditures on higher education, will most certainly grow from the two percent level of 1981 to probably more than five percent by the end of the present decade. These changes also will be accommodated within the existing higher education structures, with the addition here and there of a vice-president or a vice-provost for computing or information sciences.

The demand for computing courses in higher education will also continue to increase in spite of the continuing shortage of trained instructors in computer sciences, a shortage which the Bureau of Labor Statistics predicts will continue through 1990. Most colleges and universities have made dramatic increases in computer sciences enrollments over the past decade. The University of Wisconsin at Madison, for example, reports that it has increased computer class capacity by ten percent annually over the past several years, a figure matched at the University of Delaware over the last four years for the introductory computer sciences course. Georgia Tech, as another example, recently expanded its computing enrollments by fourteen percent according to a front page note in the *Wall Street Journal.*[2]

In the early 1960s only ten percent of America's colleges and universities had access to computers; ninety percent did by 1980 and nearly all will by the middle of this decade.[3] We have not yet reached the goal proposed in the Pierce Report of three hours per month per student of on-line time, but by the end of the 1980s we could surpass that with microcomputers alone.[4]

Problems will continue to occur, however, in the selection of computing equipment to meet divergent campus needs and in the distribution of computing resources across departments. As a step toward solving both of these problems, many universities have moved away from the totally centralized, single machine concept, to a distributed computing service. This allows a better match of resources to specialized needs, and at the same time allows a gradual introduction of new technologies. Equally important is the involvement of the faculty in planning for research and instructional computing; in most cases this increases the probability of equitable distribution of resources. Both of these directions, I feel, will be adopted by more and more colleges and universities in the coming years. A succession of blue ribbon panels have written on these matters since 1962 when the Rosser Committee on *Digital Computer Needs in Universities and Colleges* was commissioned by the National Academy of Sciences.[5] From this report, the 1967 Pierce Report,[6] and the 1981 Gillespie Report,[7] one can find predictions of almost all of the promises and issues I have just discussed. Perhaps the most astute characterization of computing ever proposed was made in the Pierce Report in 1967 when it stated that "After growing wildly for years, the field of computing now appears to be approaching its infancy."

In summary, the outer layer predicts that computers will continue to flow onto the campus through the front gate, the back gate, the chimney, and through the coal chute. They will nestle into every corner and cubby hole they can find, chew up a little more silage each year, stir up a little trouble here and there, but leave the foundation intact and the house standing a little straighter than before.

The Middle Layer

The second layer, representing a certainty level somewhere between predicting the outcome of an instant replay and predicting the height of next year's hemline, centers on three areas in which computer technology might bring dramatic benefits to higher education through alterations in structures and processes. But these changes will also be capable of doing great harm to the health and well-being of institutions and their faculties if not properly managed. First among these areas is the potential for resource sharing that advanced digital communications will provide. Colleges and universities are now competing not only for a dwindling student pool but also for decreased federal support, all in the face of continually rising costs. In a recent speech, Frank Rhodes, president of Cornell University, listed resource sharing among the first steps that colleges and universities must take to maintain their quality.[8]

Computer technology already has allowed the sharing of library sources through regional centers for on-line cataloguing (e.g., OCLC)[9] and the sharing of computer facilites through national networking (e.g., EDUNET).[10] Reductions in the cost of broadband data transmission could also aid faculty sharing through electronic blackboards and teleconferencing. Courses physically centered in one university might be attended on-line by students throughout the country. Similarly, guest lecturers, tutors, and other human resources at remote sites might be accessed on-line without the costs and inconveniences of travel. This past spring, the New Jersey Institute of Technology became the first institute of higher learning to offer a full program of continuing education via computerized conferencing. Over twenty seminars were offered via an electronic information exchange system that the institute established several years ago. In time we might see mergers of colleges and universities, using computer technology to give direct access across locations.

The second advancement that computer technology will bring to higher education is significant improvements in research facilities. Computing resources that once cost $1 million or more are now available for $15,000-$20,000, and at far lower maintenance and programming costs than ever before. Personal work stations, adaptable not only to scientific processing, but also to the needs of humanists, will become as common as typewriters are today. In addition, national and international networks will connect geographically remote colleagues, provide instant access to data banks of every imaginable flavor, and facilitate the publication of scholarly journals through on-line transmission of submissions, reviews, and perhaps even the journals themselves.

But the acceptance of such unqualified blessings is seldom without its dangers. And danger certainly confronts the utilization of computers in research, for a fascination with technology has shown itself capable of biasing scholarly judgment. This phenomenon was known even 250 years ago when Gulliver visited the Academy of Lagado. A professor there had constructed a matrix of wooden cubes whereon were affixed all the words of the language. By turning cranks, the cubes could be rotated, creating random arrangements of words. Says Swift:

> Everyone knew how laborious the usual method is of attaining to Arts and Sciences; whereas by his contrivance, the most ignorant person at a reasonable charge, and with a little bodily labour, may write books in Philosophy, Poetry, Politicks, Law, Mathematicks, and Theology, without the least assistance from Genius or Study.[11]

In the humanities in particular, where computer applications outside of word processing are relatively uncommon, the evaluation of computer-aided research is often difficult. For example, in the not too distant past a considerable amount of bland and unimaginative work on stylistics was funded and widely published, mainly because it was computer based. Promises were freely made of powerful tools for ascertaining authorship, sequencing variant texts, and for gen
erating stories by methods not too different from those employed at Lagado. But alas, time did more for the judgments of the referees than it did for the capabilities of the occupational stylisticians, and most of the claims have been mercifully forgotten.

We are in total a more technically sophisticated community of scholars today than we were twenty years ago, but we can not help but be attracted to reports produced on laser printers with right-margin justification and publication-quality typography. Nor can we totally ignore poorly written research reports that claim through computer assistance to have uncovered some new irregularity in the heart throb of a revered writer. A fascination with machines runs deep in the American soul, and the sense of accomplishment in mastering the secrets of keyboard, diskette, and printer can dull one's critical abilities. A text-processing work station in the hands of an incompetent scholar will yield incompetent scholarship, no matter how well margins are justified. The danger, however, is not in a plague of slick but vacuous publications that might be generated through personal computers, but in the diversion of scholars themselves under the false hope that a trivial idea by machine is superior to an ordinary one by hand. Whether personal work stations are energizing or stupefying in the humanities will ultimately depend on the general level of technological understanding in the field, which of course depends upon the willingness of humanists to explore and understand technology.

The third asset that might be reaped from computer technology is the facilitation of instruction. Computer technology offers a number of potential benefits to instruction, including networked access to remote resources, as sketched above, and computer-aided instruction. But with the latter application caution is highly advised. Since the 1950s the teacher-free, completely automated classroom has been a staple of the futurists creed. Millions of dollars have been spent attempting to replace teachers by computers, yet the rationale for this effort has rarely been examined seriously. There appear to be benefits for vocational education, community colleges, and continuing education from certain types of computer-aided instruction, and for colleges and universities through on-line problems sets, exams, grading, course communications, and other adjuncts to instruction; but there is little evidence that in the near future benefits will be reaped at the latter institutions from delivering completely automated courses.

Teaching is the life-blood of colleges and universities, the *sine qua non* for their primary support and for their patronage by students. Whatever its quality and volume of research, a university without competent instruction is not a university, and what competent instructors do is not easily imitated by computers. The experiments in this decade that will have the largest impact on instruction are those like the computerized conferencing project mentioned above and the SUNet Project at Stanford University, where computers and video services such as teleconferencing and public service broadcasting are being combined in a single network to facilitate both instruction and research. By the end of this decade such systems will be widely applied in higher education. These networks will also provide for faculty improvement through planning and communications tools, immediate access to films and archival material, and the ability to monitor model lessons. In this way part of the answer can be provided to a question raised by Charles Eliot in his inaugural address as president of Harvard College in 1869: "How the quality of these [faculties] can be maintained and improved."[12] To achieve this end, however, colleges and universities must focus dwindling resources on support and improvement of faculty rather than on their replacement. The time has long passed when the idea of totally automated instruction in higher education should have been chucked out. "An open mind," says Northrop Frye, "should be open at both ends, like a food pipe, and have a capacity for excretions as well as intake."[13]

The Inner Layer

My final and innermost layer of concern deals with the impact of computer technology on the very essence of the modern college or university. Clark Kerr has pointed out that 66 western institutions have survived since the year 1530 without significant alteration in form, and that 62 of these are universities.[14] Whether any universities survive the next thirty years in their present forms may depend on how well each can protect its integrity against the demands of a computer-based society. High technology has already altered some of the traditional faculty relationships in higher education. Departments that involve themselves in high technology receive the largess of private industry and the government, not only in research grants and gifts, but in consulting arrangements and positions for graduate students. Consequently, some departments have large per faculty budgets for travel, xeroxing, hourly help, and other support services, while others ration their paper clips and pencils.

This inequality might be accepted as an inevitable aberration, well-confined and benign, except that the migration of faculty to high technology centers and the deeper involvement of remaining faculty with industry (sometimes to the point of divided appointments), further reduces the ability of colleges and universities to be intellectual institutions, immune to the pressures and constraints of business and politics. A faculty that spends half of its time with industry is not a faculty that is totally free to question old truths and search out new ones. At risk is not just the integrity of the sciences, but the well-being of the arts and humanities also. The problem of utility, which Eva Brann discusses in her *Paradoxes of Education in a Republic*,[15] is being settled without discussion in favor of a commitment to the immediate needs of industry and government. With this bending, the arts and humanities are being threatened with second-class citizenship: happy, amusing folks to have around, but not ones you can depend on to help our industrial connections.

As the university becomes more and more a partner with industry and government in developing and applying computer technology, the role of the arts and humanities will diminish. Developers of computer-aided design systems, for example, are not generally interested in Plato's views on esthetics, nor Panofsky's on iconography. Recently, a consensus panel of university administrators and industrial leaders called for cooperative programs among industry, higher education, and government to strengthen computing activities in higher education.[16] Support for any goals of higher education by industry and government is generally welcomed; however, there are reasons to believe that in such an arrangement representatives of industry and government would not ignore their own views of colleges and universities in modern society, views that seldom in the past have been completely consonant with those of educators. Students have responded to this new era in American life by rushing to enroll in the high-utility programs: computer sciences, engineering, and business. Foreign language departments are withering, as are departments in the arts and humanities. The prognosis for such departments is not particularly bright.

The problems I am forecasting can all be avoided. Blue ribbon panels can call until the cows come home for consortia of university, industry, and government, but until we sign the marriage certificate, no wedding will take place. Computer technology will force us to define what we are better than we have done in the past. If we are to be contracting agencies for industry and government, let's own up now to our new role and start drawing advanced payments; but if we are to retain our independence, then we must clarify for ourselves the price we are willing to pay for little gray boxes that go beep in the night.

Computer technology is not, however, the cause of our potential problems. This technology by itself is neither productive nor disruptive; it is, rather, the insatiable appetite of society to automate, to place machines in control, that engenders our current ills. Modern society, as represented by industry and government, is attempting to absorb computer technology at a rate far in excess of what can be comfortably managed with the skills presently available. As a consequence of this mismatch, the universities, with their scientific resources, are being asked to participate more directly in satisfying contemporary needs than universities have ever done in the past. And while the price might be right, it is not paid without expectations of responsiveness.

Those outside education have already told us that we should teach COBOL and FORTRAN in our programming courses because they are the languages preferred in business and industry for software, and that we should buy certain manufacturer's machinery so we can share programs with them. In the face of these pressures, it is to the credit of our computer sciences departments that computing instruction over the past decade has moved from a utilitarian orientation to a more theoretical and, surprisingly, humanistic base. Even the high-enrollment introductory courses are beginning to stress structure and readability of programs over simple utilitarian matters.

If the marriage of microelectronics and communications benefits higher education at the end of the twentieth century, it will be because colleges and universities will have vigorously maintained a prominent place for liberal education in an information-based society. A humane technology should be as deeply rooted in history, the social sciences, and philosophy as it is in physics and mathematics. We need neither the Delphic oracle nor Nick the Greek to tell us what will happen if we ignore the former and over-indulge the latter. Dewey recognized this same problem just before the middle of this century when he wrote, "The problem of securing to the liberal arts college its due function in democratic society is that of seeing to it that the technical subjects which are now socially necessary acquire a humane direction."[17]

This same need exists today in colleges and universities—to ensure a humane, intellectual base to technical subjects and particularly to computer sciences. If our emphasis for computer technology in the future is not balanced between the mathematical/scientific components of computing and the historical, sociological, cultural, and political components, we will have little to distinguish ourselves from the vocational schools and technological institutes. One of the most important impacts of computer technology on higher education should therefore be an increased presence of liberal studies in the technical curriculum and a wider utilization of technology to demonstrate the enduring values of the liberal arts. Under these conditions colleges and universities can continue to be true both to themselves and to society.

NOTES

1. R. G. Gillespie, *Computing and Higher Education: An Accidental Revolution*, Final Report, NSF Grant SED-7823790 (Seattle, Washington: University of Washington, 1981).

2. *The Wall Street Journal*, 1 September 1983.

3. Gillespie, *Computing and Higher Education*.

4. President's Science Advisory Committee, *Computers in Higher Education* (Washington, D.C.: U.S. Government Printing Office, 1967).

5. National Academy of Sciences, *Digital Computer Needs in Universities and Colleges*, Publication 1233 (Washington, D.C., 1966).

6. President's Science Advisory Committee, *Computers in Higher Education*.

7. Gillespie, *Computing and Higher Education*.

8. F. Rhodes, *Cornell Alumni News* (September 1983), pp. 25-28.

9. (On-line Computing Library Center) is a nonprofit organization that maintains an international network for tracing, acquiring, and cataloging books and other library materials. Originally called the Ohio Center for Library Cataloging, OCLC has recently expanded its services to include arranging of interlibrary loans and other library services.

10. EDUNET is a national network of colleges and universities formed to encourage sharing of computer resources in higher education. The operation of EDUNET is overseen by the Planning Council Computing in Education and Research, which is a nonprofit organzation based in Princeton, New Jersey.

11. J. Swift, *Gulliver's Travels* (New York: The Heritage Press, 1940), p. 201.

12. *The Inaugural Address of Charles William Eliot as President of Harvard College,* October 19, 1869 (Cambridge, Massachusetts: Harvard University Press, 1969).

13. N. Frye, *The Great Code* (New York: Harcourt Brace Jovanovich, 1982).

14. Cited in Rhodes, *Cornell Alumni News.*

15. E. T. H. Brann, *Paradoxes of Education in a Republic* (Chicago: University of Chicago Press, 1979).

16. Gillespie, *Computing and Higher Education.*

17. J. Dewey, "The Problems of the Liberal Arts Colleges," *American Scholar* 13 (1944), p. 393.

Virginia B. Smith

Creativity and Order: Liberal Education in Transition

E. B. White once wrote, "I arise in the morning torn between a desire to improve the world and to enjoy the world. This makes it hard to plan the day." Whenever I turn my attention to the subject of the future of liberal arts, I am also torn by competing desires. It is not a coincidence that I personally see liberal education as the truest and best form of undergraduate education and I believe that it is practiced in its highest form at small- to moderate-sized, selective, independent, liberal arts colleges. That is why I am at Vassar. But I have an equally strong belief that liberal education is too valuable to be the special privilege of the educational elite, whether those elite are determined by a meritocratic standard or a socioeconomic class. I want to find ways to make liberal education available to all citizens and to have it infuse education in a range of settings.

I share with my colleagues the desire to perfect liberal education within that sensitive four-year age period, between seventeen and twenty-one, but I am equally aware of the fact that the goals of liberal education are such that they cannot be attained within a lifetime, let alone four years.

I, too, wish the content through which liberal education is achieved to be selected with great care and with certainty that the content will have the richness, style, scope, and discipline of thought that will help achieve the aims of liberal education for the learner. I desire even more strongly, however, that the aims of a liberal education be achieved whatever the content. These aims are usually expressed not as bodies of knowledge, but as sets of abilities, skills, attitudes, and values.

I, too, desire a population educated in a common culture and having shared values, but I desire even more strongly that we not exclude the additional cultures and emerging values of an increasingly pluralistic society.

These competing desires create tensions within all institutions of higher education, but probably they are most intense in our liberal arts colleges, which have long been the bastions of liberal education, and in those disciplines that we normally refer to as the liberal arts and sciences, although far less in the social sciences and sciences than in the humanities. The future of the liberal arts disciplines, the liberal arts colleges, and liberal education will be determined by the way in which we balance the competing desires just mentioned.

There is, of course, the usual difficulty about terms. We have as much miscommunication about this subject as we have communication, because everyone uses the terms differently. Liberal arts is frequently used to refer to specific disciplines, usually thought of as an expanded trivium and quadrivium. It also is used to refer to certain colleges that have curricula more or less limited to these subjects. Most of these colleges, however, are committed in their statements of mission and purpose to liberal education. The liberal arts and sciences are the liberal arts colleges' paths to liberal education. They believe, and I do also, that these disciplines are the most effective subjects for the purpose of liberal education. Liberal arts and sciences and liberal education are not, therefore, interchangeable. But in our history and practice, they are very much intertwined. As a fervent supporter of liberal education, naturally I have my own goals for it. Liberal education is that education which not only liberates the mind, but empowers the individual to function in many roles in a complex society.

The Freedom to Dream

Each of us wishes to feel, in this vast anonymous universe, that our lives will make a difference. Many of us do not wish simply to be acted upon, we wish to act. Action is becoming more and more difficult in a society so complex, so fluid, and so impersonal. We yearn to experience the sense of dignity that comes from experiencing one's own humanity. Liberal arts education speaks to that need. It enables us to feel part of the millions of years of human struggle. It allows us to rejoice in the exploits of an Eleanor of Aquitaine or the genius of a Leonardo da Vinci. It gives us something to strive toward and someone to strive with. It liberates us from parochialism, ignorance, and fear, and arms us with the courage to be, the confidence to do. It gives us the freedom to dream, to dare to be somebody.

As such, a liberal arts education is one of our finest creations. It is hard to imagine a more necessary activity for a free people hoping to shape a peaceful, prosperous republic in a world of war, prejudice, poverty, superstition, and evil. It is ironic that there is so much despair in higher education about the future of liberal arts, just when it is so supremely important to us, more than at any other time in our history.

Liberal Education Not Static

Even though the need for it is growing, education in the humanities does appear to be in decline. In higher education, the decline seems to have begun in the early seventies. In 1971, there were 57,124 students receiving bachelor's degrees who had majored in English; by 1979, that number had dropped to 27,956. The story is similar for history, modern languages, and music. In 1976, according to the National Center for Educational Statistics, there were more than 346,000 bachelor's degrees awarded in the liberal arts. In the spring of 1980, the number had dropped to fewer than 296,000, despite an increase in college enrollments.

At the same time, degrees in engineering rose by one-half; degrees in business nearly doubled; and degrees in computer science nearly tripled. Clearly, a shift of preferences among our students is taking place. More of them are exchanging Shakespeare and history for electronics and FORTRAN.

This change has required new resources at traditional liberal arts colleges and is compelling resource allocations at many major state universities. It has also led to massive defenses of liberal education as something useful for careers, to the creation of commissions on the importance of foreign languages, and to the desire on many campuses to return to distribution requirements or some form of a core curriculum.

It is important to realize that this is an old struggle. Renaissance universities were torn between training for such professions as the clergy, law, and medicine, on the one hand; and the study of languages, astronomy, literature, and philosophy, on the other. What we know as "liberal education" has wended its way through the centuries like a chameleon, taking on the coloration of each age and society. The Renaissance scholar Petrus Paulus Vergerius described the liberal arts this way: "We call those studies *liberal* which are worthy of a free man [or woman]; those studies by which we attain and practice virtue and wisdom; that education which calls forth, trains, and develops those highest gifts of body and mind which ennoble men [and women]."[1] Over the centuries, more people have become free men and women. In this nation within the last century, we doubled the percentage of persons in our population who would be called free, and more of these free persons have been admitted to higher education.

How can we characterize the forces that led to the decline of the liberal arts and sciences? The answer heard most frequently is that the reversal has been caused by factors outside our campuses, such as the wavering economy, the increased number of people in the work force, the new difficulties in getting jobs, and decreased support from the federal government. These are surely powerful contributing factors.

When did this decline begin? If we look at a somewhat longer period, from 1962 to 1979, there has been no decline in students majoring in English, history, music, or modern languages, although the increase for these disciplines was less than the increase in total bachelor's degrees. Only mathematics, philosophy, and physics either stayed almost level or declined over this longer period. All showed a decline, as mentioned earlier, in the period from 1971 to 1979. A lot happened in higher education in the two decades from 1960 to 1979. All bachelor's degrees earned increased by 143 percent; but those earned by women rose by 235 percent, while those earned by men rose only 115 percent. By 1979, 67 percent of all bachelor's degrees were earned at public institutions contrasted with only 56 percent in 1962. A lot was going on in this period and particularly from 1967 to 1972. Pointing to external forces seems far too simple to incorporate the impact of all the changes that occurred within higher education itself. Intensive democratization with efforts toward true equity had found its way into the institution. Women and minorities now inside the doors made their selections among disciplines. There was profound discontent with the quality of teaching. The full story of the forces at work in that brief period has yet to be written. One thing we know did happen—we began a redefinition of what we call liberal education. This was, of course, not the first time.

Do the fields that appear to be declining make greater demands on the backgrounds of beginning students? We think of the study of humanities as providing an understanding of our rich cultural heritage. But does even undertaking a study of them require some basic cultural understanding? Are they based to a greater extent than the social sciences and sciences on assumptions about values and perspectives that are foreign to many of today's college students? Even skills so fundamental to the humanities as reading and writing may depend on some threshold of cultural literacy. As English professor E. D. Hirsch, Jr., has written, "Raising reading and writing levels will depend far less on our methods of instruction . . . than on the specific contents of our school curricula." What he and other researchers in the field of reading and writing techniques have discovered is that the content of education and the literate skills of a society are inextricably linked. "A certain amount of shared, canonical knowledge," Hirsch says, "is inherently necessary to a literate democracy."[2]

Those faculty members who are themselves highly specialized have developed a kind of tunnel vision that makes it difficult for them to see the broader implications in their fields of study and thus become unable to make the connections required for liberally educating their students. Many of our colleges and universities reinforce this specialization by rewarding the most specialized researchers, not the most energizing, broadly educated teachers. If this is part of the problem, a return to distribution requirements or a core curriculum will not improve the situation. It may simply send more people into technical training or other forms of education that do not include assumptions that the students already have a context for their higher learning.

It is, perhaps, the ultimate cop-out to say that students are turning their backs on liberal education because of a stampede toward vocationalism. Certainly that force is present, but we should remember that seventy percent of freshmen entering four-year colleges and universities say they want to gain a general education. That is just about the same percentage that say they want to earn a bachelor's degree and only a little lower than that of those who say they are going to college to get a better job. In other words, students have avoided the false dichotomy that characterizes so many higher education conversations—between general education and career education. Students want both, and, of course, that is possible.

Another interpretation could be that the sharp rise in humanities selection in the sixties was because students saw career possibilities, primarily teaching, in the humanities. By the early seventies, some students were disenchanted with higher education and did not think of making their careers in it. In the decade before, professors were very successful in urging their best students to follow in their footsteps. Later, the national discussion of demographics and the state of education made teaching less attractive. Thus, a certain portion of those in the humanities were there for career reasons in the first place. If we are going to blame career choices for the decline, we should also credit them for some of the increase to the peak in the early seventies.

New conditions require a rethinking of liberal education and the role of the existing fields of humanities as subjects through which the aims of liberal education may be achieved. Those teaching in the liberal arts, with their strong liberal education tradition, should be the most capable of developing the changes needed. After all, liberal education has as an aim the ability to cope with change, to understand the past, not just for itself, but as a foundation for the present and surely as a path to the future. Can we afford to fail in demonstrating those very abilities that are our stated goals? We teach our students not to be bound by the limitations of particular facts, but to keep their eyes on purpose; we should do the same.

Future Linked to Experiment in Democracy

The future of liberal education will be determined by the way we balance or resolve the competing desires mentioned earlier. The choices that are to be made, will be, I believe, basically political in nature. We think educational decisions are made on the basis of educational philosophy or expertise, but these choices are so tied to our political (and I don't mean Republican or Democratic) philosophy that we cannot ignore their importance. The future of liberal education is the future of America's experiment in democracy. The changes I see are based on my own hopes for succeeding in that experiment. The first two that I will mention are likely to happen whether we wish them to or not. The remaining are those that I believe should happen, but will not unless we take deliberate action to accomplish them.

I suspect the most fundamental change in liberal arts education in the coming years will be the movement away from thinking of the liberal arts principally as a set of courses that students take in the first two or three years of a four-year college education and toward the idea that the liberal arts are part of education at every level. Liberal education is not solely a curriculum, but an attitude, a way of learning, a lifelong commitment.

I believe we shall see more liberal arts components in our secondary schools and our business schools, in adult education and postretirement education, in two-year colleges and graduate schools. It must happen to a greater extent at the high school level if we are to have students who wish to study humanities at the college level. In any case, liberal education is too important to be limited to the four years in a college or university. We know that the baccalaureate degree is not the mark of an educated person. It is a license to practice a lifetime of liberal education. Like diamonds, a liberal education is forever.

Nor should liberal education be confined to the five percent of our young people who have the good fortune to attend our best liberal arts institutions. The future of liberal education will increasingly lie with its incorporation within every kind of educational activity, including television, records, and films. Liberal education is a program for life, not just an undergraduate package.

A second change will be the growth of efforts to make the teaching of liberal arts subjects more consistent with the aims of liberal education, more active and energizing. Critics of the liberal arts like to characterize these studies as aristocratic, appropriate for a life of leisure, and self-indulgent because they focus on individual self-development rather than the public use of knowledge. Some famous proponents of liberal education like Mark Van Doren have accepted this accusation and argue that a democracy cannot be great without more aristocratic thinking and reflection. As Van Doren put it, "What was once for the few must now be for the many. . . . Liberal education in the modern world must aim at the generosity of nature, must work to make the aristocrat, the man of grace, the person, as numerous as fate allows."[3]

Few will argue with the idea that democracy will be preserved only if it contains generous portions of excellence, what Jefferson called a "natural" aristocracy based on merit, achievement, and character. One goal of the liberal arts, after all, is to inspire nobility of purpose and thought. Perhaps this is aristocratic in tone, but then aristocrats are defined as the ruling class; in a democracy we are all, in one way or another, in the ruling class.

A third major change which I believe to be necessary is far greater attention to the values implicit in the traditional courses that provide the substance of liberal education. The physicist F. Capra asserts that we are in the midst of a great change in values. This makes liberal education, which is supposed to transmit cultural values, particularly difficult. Capra writes that we are in "a transition of planetary dimensions. As individuals, as a society, as a civilization, and as a planetary ecosystem, we are reaching the turning point." He goes on to say,

> Cultural transformation of this magnitude and depth cannot be prevented. They should not be opposed but, on the contrary, should be welcomed. . . . What we need, to prepare ourselves for the great transition we are about to enter, is a deep reexamination of the main premises and values of our culture, a rejection of those conceptual models that have outlived their usefulness, and a new recognition of some of the values discarded in previous periods of our cultural history.[4]

How will we teach philosophy in the future when the classical philosophers, consistent with the value of their times, are both sexist and nondemocratic? Will history in our future liberal education be as concerned about chronicling the events and impacts of women, blacks, and families as they have been about the major political and military events? Similar questions can be raised about other traditional fields. Whether we recognize it or not, liberal education inculcates values, and to the extent that the values in the classroom refuse to recognize the emergence of new values outside the classroom, liberal education will fail.

The heart of any liberal education is the faculty. While liberal education should expand in the future beyond our colleges and universities, it will continue to be in higher education that many persons receive their most intense exposure to liberal learning. So the faculty are a determining force. Teaching will be central. But the blunt fact today is that we have fewer and fewer teachers who can educate liberally. There are more and more professors who take teaching positions at universities in order to have a base from which to engage in research. While America's researchers are, to be sure, a national asset, we must come to see that professors who can teach young people in the liberal arts are also a national asset. We should review the preparation, hiring, and rewards of the academic profession.

A fourth change that will be required, if liberal education is to have a bright future, will be to give greater attention to providing advanced liberal education for our prospective teachers. We may also require greater interaction between universities and undergraduate colleges, because it is in the latter that we have given teaching for liberal education a more central role.

A fifth change will be the addition of some new general abilities to the aims of liberal education. The new abilities are those needed to liberate and empower change at the margins as society changes. Our students will need to learn how to have tolerance for ambiguity combined with the skill to be precise when needed; to be flexible and adaptable while maintaining a personal core of integrity; and to deal with complexity without reducing it to overly simplistic characterizations. These are not easy educational aims. Today, we are, as a nation, more mobile, more fragmented in our group allegiances, more expectant of change, and more randomly informed than ever before. Learning to live in this kind of society, learning to make choices in it, will place new demands on liberal education.

Everything Correlates

The new liberal arts curriculum will, of necessity, have a somewhat different shape. The interrelationships between disciplines may become as important as the disciplines. The new scholarship, particularly on women, and in sciences such as biochemistry and genetics, may require reshaping the boundaries and the very assumptions of our current disciplines. But above all, the liberal arts education of the future must be grounded in *connections*. As two wise Vassar cartoonists taught us, the aim of liberal education is to show that "Everything Correlates." In my view this is crucial. As we move away from our linear, mechanical, progressive view of the world to a greater sense of the interdependence of all life, we are developing a livelier appreciation of the connectedness of things. People and nature, past and present, other cultures and ours, government and citizens, the humanities and the sciences—all these and many more connections are beginning to loom larger in our attitudes. And perhaps most important are the new connections that must be created between science and the humanities. Many of today's most difficult human and humane questions will grow out of our scientific developments. Such connections have long been a staple of the liberal arts, which have perennially opened our eyes to the ties between our economic life and our philosophy, our religion and our art, our morality and our poetry. Because in our age of specialization, as Yeats said, "things fall apart," this graceful and persistent leaning toward life's connections is no small thing. Liberal education will be the vital cord of the future, binding us, uniting us, keeping us whole.

Finally, liberal education of the future must stress creativity and imagination, not only in its students but in its proponents. If, increasingly, we will have to invent our own futures, like jazz musicians invent their own melodic variations, we will need to keep our eyes on what is indispensable in liberal education—its purposes. In tying liberal education to a specific core of contents, or to a single place of learning, or to a fixed stratum of our young people, we have welded some false bondings. We will need a common purpose more than a common content. To educate a student population whose backgrounds and ages are more widely varied than ever before, we will need different strategies and different materials with which to teach. But the purpose—that of liberating people from ignorance and provincialism and of empowering them to create boldly and live gladly in a vast, impersonal solar system—will remain the same.

When we are in the middle of a transition, as we are today in liberal education, we are too likely to feel that decline has set in, that we no longer value what is important. In pain and in fear we try to recapture what was. But what is important may also be shifting. Looking backward certainly has its value, but even that process must be tempered by our knowledge of the present and our anticipation of the future. As Gertrude Stein said, "And how do you look backward. By looking forward. And what do they see. As they look forward. They see what they had to do before they could look backward. And there we have it all."

NOTES

1. Pietro Paolo Vergerio, *De Ingenius Moribus,* tr. W. H. Woodward in *Vittorino De Feltre and Other Humanist Educators* (New York: Teachers College, Columbia University, 1963), pp. 93-119.

2. E. D. Hirsch, Jr., "Cultural Literacy," *American Scholar* 52:2 (Spring 1983), pp. 159-169.

3. Mark Van Doren, *Liberal Education* (New York: Henry Holt and Co., 1943), p. 31

4. F. Capra, *The Turning Point: Science, Society, and the Rising Culture* (New York: Simon and Schuster, 1982).

Jan H. Blits

The Search for Ends: Liberal Education and the Modern University

Does liberal education belong in the modern American university? Is the university's obligation to research conducive to, or even compatible with, its commitment to liberal education? Should the university continue its efforts to provide liberal education, or should it concentrate on research and vocational training and leave liberal education to traditional liberal arts colleges?

The view prevailing today, and the one that has prevailed since the establishment of the modern American university a century ago, is that strong research contributes to good teaching and is perhaps even indispensable to it. "A university which is not a place of research will not long continue to be a place of good teaching," argued Charles W. Eliot.[1] "It is best of all if teaching is combined with live research, with original work that is still in progress," observed Herbert Butterfield. "Only those who are continually probing into the body of their knowledge, and trying to unthink last year's thoughts, can convey along with the information, the thrill of the real quest for knowledge."[2] Going a step further, Alfred North Whitehead, arguing that research and teaching are inseparable because they enhance each other, explained how "the two functions of education and research meet together in a university." "Do you want your teachers to be imaginative?" he asked rhetorically.

Then encourage them to research. Do you want your researchers to be imaginative? Then bring them into intellectual sympathy with the young at the most eager, imaginative period of life, when intellects are just entering upon their mature discipline. Make your researchers explain themselves to active minds, plastic and with the work before them; make your young students crown their period of intellectual acquisition by some minds gifted with experience of intellectual adventure. Education is discipline for the adventure of life; research is intellectual adventure; and the universities should be homes of adventure shared in common by young and old.[3]

In short, the prevalent belief is that teaching and research are both done best when done in combination.

Yet, right from the beginning, this sanguine view has also been sharply disputed, by some in the name of research, by others in the name of teaching. Arguing that a university should be devoted entirely to advanced research and graduate training, Daniel Coit Gilman told the Johns Hopkins University Board of Trustees that under his presidency the institution would promote "scholarship of the first order, and this by only offering the kind of instruction to advanced students which other universities offer in their post-graduate courses, and leaving the kind of work now done by undergraduates to be done elsewhere."[4] And Abraham Flexner, concerned that the dual functions of the university produce a confusion of purpose that degrades research, argued that "the pursuit of science and scholarship belongs to the university," but not undergraduate instruction, which "must not be permitted to distract the university."[5] On the other side, Robert M. Hutchins, attacking the quality of undergraduate teaching in a research-oriented institution, wrote:

A university can be a university without doing any teaching. It cannot be one without doing any research. But there is an essential conflict between teaching and research. Education is synthetic and generalized. Research is analytical and detailed. Education is becoming more generalized. Research is becoming more specialized. The college teacher, after intensive training in a minute field of physics, is expected to teach a general course in the natural sciences.[6]

As early as the turn of the century, Henry S. Pritchett, president of the Carnegie Foundation for the Advancement of Teaching, observed that "the university, as at present organized, has two entirely different functions," from which he concluded that "Whatever may be the advantages of combination of the college and the university into one organization, I am convinced that it would be of immense value to the educational system of the country if a few strong universities could be established, with generous facilities for social intercourse, but without undergraduate colleges."[7]

It is important to realize that the relation between teaching and research became an issue in American education only with the rise of the modern American university. Before the Morrill Land-Grant Act (1862), Eliot's presidency at Harvard (1869–1909), and the establishment of such institutions as Cornell (1868), Johns Hopkins (1876), Chicago (1891) and Stanford (1891), among other seminal events, institutions of higher learning in this country (even those calling themselves universities) had only one purpose, namely, to teach. Research was not expected, let alone required, of professors. The professor's only function was to instruct his students. In doing that, he did his job. It is true that the professor was also expected to perform a number of activities outside the classroom, but all of these additional activities centered on his primary function as a teacher. Most important, none had anything to do with research or scholarship. The teacher was one person; the researcher, another. The transmission of knowledge belonged to one sort of institution (colleges); its advancement, to another (so-called learned societies).

Why were these earlier institutions able to ignore research and limit the faculty's function to teaching? The reason has to do with the aims of traditional college education and the kind of knowledge those aims entail. The early college rested on the proposition that there are certain fundamental truths and skills that every educated person should possess. Its purpose was to guide its students to the recovery of those truths while at the same time teaching them how to learn; to lay a foundation for, not to provide a student with, specialized training. Jeremiah Day, writing in the Yale Report of 1828, carefully distinguished the collegiate curriculum and purpose from that of the newly proposed comprehensive university with its departmental organization and elective system. The collegiate plan, with its prescribed course of study and emphasis on the classics,

> is far from embracing *every thing* which the student will ever have occasion to learn. The object is not to *finish* his education; but to lay the foundation, and to advance as far in rearing the superstructure, as the short period of his residence here will admit. If he acquires here a thorough knowledge of the principles of science, he may then, in a great measure, educate himself. He has, at least, been taught *how* to learn.[8]

Because such knowledge does not depend on advances in research but remains the same over time, traditional collegiate education could ignore research or scholarship and concentrate only on teaching.

In sharp contrast to the broad aims of the traditional college, the aims of the modern American university are immediately and directly practical. So is the kind of knowledge that it teaches. "We have in this country one hundred and twenty colleges, forty-two theological seminaries, and forty-seven law schools," wrote Francis Wayland in his famous 1850 Report to the Corporation of Brown University, "and yet we have not a single institution designed to furnish the agriculturist, the manufacturer, the mechanic, or the merchant with the education that will prepare him for the profession to which his life is to be devoted." Wayland, a leader of the mid-nineteenth-century movement to establish the so-called "true" or "real" university in America, thus urged replacing the prescribed collegiate curriculum with a radically expanded course of study, based on an elective system, and adapted to the particular needs and interests of each segment of society. "We must carefully survey the wants of the various classes of the community in our own vicinity, and adapt our courses of instruction, not for the benefit of one class, but for the benefit of all classes."[9] In the words of Ezra Cornell: "I would found an institution where any person can find instruction in any study."[10]

In a chapter entitled "Why the Americans Are More Addicted to Practice than to Theoretical Science,"[11] Tocqueville distinguishes among three kinds of science. The first comprises the most highly theoretial principles and abstract notions whose application is either unknown or very remote; the second is composed of those general truths still belonging to pure theory, but leading nevertheless directly to practical results; the third is made up of methods of application and means of execution. The second and particularly the third are characteristic of the modern American university, as Wayland exemplifies when he writes:

> The moral conditions being equal, the progress of a nation in wealth, happiness, and refinement, is measured by the universality of its knowledge of the laws of nature, and its skill in adapting these laws to the purposes of man. Civilization is advancing, and it can only advance in the line of the useful arts. It is, therefore, of the greatest national importance to spread broadcast over the community, that knowledge, by which alone the useful arts can be multiplied and perfected.[12]

Such knowledge is, as Wayland also indicates, essentially cumulative or progressive. It advances over time by proceeding to make new discoveries that supersede previous ones on which it builds. Such knowledge is therefore inherently connected to research. Jefferson suggested this connection, as well as its underlying Baconian spirit, in stating the advantages to be expected from the proposed University of Virginia:

> . . . it cannot be but that each generation succeeding to the knowledge acquired by all those who preceded it, adding to it their own acquisitions & discoveries, and handing the mass down for successive & constant accumulation, must advance the knowledge & well-being of mankind; not *infinitely*, as some have said, but

indefinitely, and to a term which no one can fix or foresee. Indeed we need look back half a century, to times which many now living remember well, and see the wonderful advances in the sciences and arts which have been made within that period. Some of these have rendered the elements themselves subservient to the purposes of man, have harnessed them to the yoke of his labours, and effected the great blessings of moderating his own, of accomplishing what was beyond his feeble force, & of extending the comforts of life to a much enlarged circle, to those who had before known its necessaries only.[13]

Research thus becomes an integral part of the university's purpose and structure when education focuses on the acquisition of technical knowledge. And as the university's function changes, so does the professor's. The professor can no longer be only an instructor. As a member of an institution that combines research and teaching, he, unlike his collegiate counterpart, must become a researcher as well as a teacher.

The effects of this development have been momentous. As early as the turn of the century, William Rainey Harper, president of the University of Chicago, could announce gladly that "The spirit of research, once hardly recognized in our educational world, is now the controlling spirit." Woodrow Wilson, then a professor at Princeton, could observe approvingly that at least at his alma mater, Johns Hopkins, "the discovery and dissemination of new truths were conceded a rank superior to mere instruction."[14] Where research is granted a rank superior to teaching, it is hardly surprising to find professors, particularly if they happen to be distinguished researchers, who depreciate the importance of undergraduate instruction. The attitude of E. L. Thorndike, Columbia's eminent psychologist and a founder of modern educational psychology, may have been extreme but is not unrepresentative. "One day just before noon he [Thorndike] glanced at the clock and remarked, 'I must give a lecture in five minutes. It would be fifty percent better if I spent this time in preparation. But let's compute another coefficient of correlation.' "[15]

Concentration upon research has also had a profound if more

subtle effect on universities themselves. While the universities, in contrast to some of their faculty, are not indifferent to good undergraduate teaching, they are nonetheless constitutionally inclined to take it for granted. While perhaps only a naive undergraduate would make the mistake of assuming that a professor is a strong researcher just because he is a good teacher, research-oriented universities are apt to assume that if someone is a strong researcher he must also be a good teacher. Just as they require for appointment the Ph.D., a research degree, so they also tend to infer much of the quality of a professor's teaching from the quality of his research. Moreover, while good teaching and strong research both make considerable demands on a professor's time, universities seldom reward them equally. Every complex merit system is apt to contain a characteristic bias, and the university promotion and tenure system is no exception. Accomplishments in research weigh far more heavily than ones in teaching. Thus, even a professor who truly loves teaching may find himself stinting the time he gives it, particularly if he also happens to love his research. In setting its promotion criteria, the university necessarily determines its faculty's priorities.

If the problems concerning undergraduate education as a whole at the modern American university are largely circumstantial, the major tensions pertaining specifically to liberal education and university research are inherent to the two activities themselves. They arise from differences between the basic concerns of liberal education and university research and from the kinds of knowledge these two activities pursue.

The fundamental differences are usually—but incorrectly, I believe—posed in terms of the conflicting demands of specialization and generality or breadth. Undergraduate education, it is said, should unify or synthesize knowledge, providing students with an integrated understanding of knowledge as a whole and of the complex interdependence and interrelationships of the various disciplines. Students should be brought to see the general foundation of knowledge, the common threads of learning, the common ground for all the parts of knowledge. Such a purpose was indeed intended by at least some, if not most, of the proponents of the "true" university in America. For Henry P. Tappan, for example, the university's unity was crucial. "The very idea of a University," he wrote,

> is that of concentrating books and apparatus, and learned men in one place. All branches of human learning are cognate, and require for their successful prosecution, cordial co-operation and mutual support. Nay, they are logically interdependent, so that to separate them would be to render their development impossible. The relations existing between the branches of knowledge symbolize the relations of the professors and students in these branches. Together they form a learned society, the members of which operate upon each other by the communication of ideas in daily converse, by the force of example, and by the excitement of noble and generous competition.[16]

Tappan's idea of a university was inspired by the German university model, where research was largely confined to the first of Tocqueville's three grades of science: pure theory. The American university, however, is organized for the sort of practical research that requires a high degree of specialization. Modeled on Baconian science, it divides the intellectual world, which Bacon appropriately renamed the "intellectual globe," into numerous areas or fields—literally, "departments"—in order to conduct well-defined, highly specialized research that leads to the advancement of knowledge and the practical benefits that come from it. Moreover, this division of intellectual labor produces a further narrowing effect as the kind of research the university conducts is concerned largely with solving problems. The researchers and their students are trained to think in terms of analysis, that is, to construe intellectual matters as problems resolvable into smallest parts. "Divide each of the difficulties . . . into as many parts as possible and as is required to solve them best," said Descartes.[17] Thus, the proponents of general education argue, the university's emphasis on practical research separates precisely what undergraduate education should draw together. As both the child and the parent of specialization, the emphasis necessarily fragments learning, producing well-trained specialists for whom everything outside their narrow fields is quite literally a closed book.

On the other side, defenders of specialization, particularly in the natural sciences, often rest their case on two points, one positive, the other negative. The positive point is summed up well by Harry D. Gideonse when he quotes Flexner against Hutchins:

> The danger that Mr. Hutchins professes to see in scientific specialization is well answered by Mr. Flexner: "It is fashionable to rail at specialization; but the truth is that specialization has brought us to the point we have reached, and more highly specialized intelligence will alone carry us further."[18]

While Gideonse agrees with Hutchins on the danger of specialization lapsing into gross vocationalism, he argues that of the two functions of a university—the transmission of knowledge and its advancement—the latter is the more important, for unless knowledge is constantly advanced "it tends to become static and authoritarian and fails to keep pace with changing reality and emerging problems."[19] No specialization, no progress. The negative point is that the goal of universal knowledge is no longer possible. "As science advances, it invariably becomes more specialized, and it is, of course, inevitable that no person can have all the knowledge of all the specialists," Gideonse writes.

> It is recognized that, as Mr. Hutchins says, "neither the world nor knowledge of it is arbitrarily divided up as universities are." Whereas in earlier periods of human history a single mind could comprehend all that was known, precisely because the stock of knowledge was less extensive, in our day one of the measures of scientific maturity is that "we have become increasingly and painfully aware of our abysmal ignorance. No scientist, fifty years ago, could have realized that he was as ignorant as all first-rate scientists now know themselves to be." The abysmal ignorance to which Mr. Flexner refers is, of course, an inevitable concomitant of the expanding horizon of science.[20]

According to such argument, the ideal of the so-called universal man is simply a romantic relic from a simpler past.

It seems to me that both sides in this continuing controversy are correct up to a point, but misconstrue and obscure the real problem. The proponents of general education are correct in saying that undergraduate education should be concerned with knowledge in its fundamental unity, but they seem to mistake broad coverage for true unity. A university student can study in one subject or department after another and still come no closer to learning the fundamental unity of knowledge. Once the intellectual world has been divided up into the various disciplines for the convenience of research, there is nothing remaining to reunite it. All the parts may be there, but they no longer add up to a genuine whole. The Baconian prejudgment underlying the division—that true knowledge is instrumental knowledge—eliminates the possibility of genuine unity as it frees science or knowledge from the philosophical search for ends. In so doing, it renders all of the parts of knowledge merely parts. True knowledge becomes the knowledge of media or means—knowledge of processes and procedures, of methods and techniques, of relationships and formulas, of trends and developments, of how to solve problems, of how things operate, of how to produce or effect something:

> *Science* is the knowledge of consequences, and dependence of one fact upon another: by which, out of that we can presently do, we know how to do something else when we will, or the like another time; because when we see how any thing comes about, upon what causes, and by what manner; when the like causes come into our power, we see how to make it produce the like effects.[21]

General education thus seeks the fundamental unity of knowledge on the wrong level. In effect, it ignores the art of architecture while seeking the unity of housebuilding on the level of, or among, the subordinate and specialized arts of bricklaying, plumbing, carpentry, and so on.

Gideonse is correct when he says that specialization has

brought us to where we are (at least in the sciences), and that further specialization will carry us still further. But, in addition to his overlooking the seminal contributions of nonspecialists such as Bacon, Descartes, Leibniz, Newton, and others in this development, he makes the fundamental mistake of supposing that specialized knowledge can be intellectually self-sufficient and that the knowledge of means or of methods can be completely independent of the end it serves. "Instead of merely contemplating Knowledge and the Good," he says scornfully of traditional liberal education, a better education is one that teaches "the techniques by which Knowledge and the Good may be made more secure"[22]—in other words, one which takes its own goals for granted. Every useful art—every kind of technique or technology—ultimately takes the goodness of its own end for granted. Medical knowledge, for example, teaches us how to restore or preserve health but not why health, or indeed life, is good. That is something it merely assumes. Guided by some opinion or knowledge lying beyond its particular sphere of competence, medical knowledge, like every other form of useful knowledge, ultimately serves an end whose goodness it cannot explain but merely assumes. Its knowledge is regional, not comprehensive. It needs to be supplemented or guided by a rigorous study of ends.

Gideonse makes a similar mistake when he argues against the possibility of a universal man today. It is no doubt true that no one today can have the knowledge of all the specialties, but no one ever could know everything. The universal man was never thought to possess encyclopedic knowledge. He did not coast along every shore and explore every field on the Baconian globe. "Much learning does not teach understanding," wrote Heraclitus.[23] The universal man was, to be sure, interested in specialized studies. But he concerned himself with biology, physics, politics, language, psychology, mathematics, or whatever because of the light such studies shed on universal questions such as What is knowledge? What is justice? What is science? What is nature? and What is truth? The knowledge he sought was concerned with matters belonging to no one discipline but underlying all of them and giving knowledge its fundamental unity.[24] Contrary to the shared supposition of general and specialized education, the unity of knowledge is vertical, not horizontal.

Liberal education, with which general education is often confused,[25] is concerned with just such knowledge of ends. In its original sense, liberal education means the education of free human beings. It means the sort of education that pertains to freedom or to the free (*liberi*).[26] What is meant by freedom or free human beings, however, is—and always has been—ambiguous. In ancient times, to be free meant to be one's own person, to be no one else's instrument or tool. But it also meant to be free from the bonds of utility, to be engaged in activities that are ends in themselves and not merely means to further ends. Liberal education was thus understood in contrast to vocational education, both of which, however, were seen as having a proper place in life. "All of life," writes Aristotle,

> is divided between work and leisure, and between war and peace, and of our activities some are necessary and useful and others are noble. The same preference must be exercised in these matters as in regard to the parts of the soul and their activities—war must be for the sake of peace, work for the sake of leisure, and necessary and useful things for the sake of noble things. The statesman must legislate with a view to all these things—the parts of the soul and their activities, and particularly those that are better and are ends, and similarly with regard to the ways of life and the choice of actions. For men must be capable of engaging in work and war, but still more capable of remaining at peace and at leisure. And they must be able to do necessary and useful things, but still more they must be able to do the noble things. Accordingly, it is with these aims in view that they should be educated when they are still children and at the later ages in life that require education.[27]

And, he concludes:

> It is therefore not difficult to see that the young must be taught those useful arts that are indispensably necessary; but, those

> pursuits that are liberal having been distinguished from those
> that are illiberal, it is clear that they should not be taught all the
> useful arts, and that they must participate in such among them as
> will not make the participant a philistine.[28]

Liberal education is thus education toward activities that are ends
in themselves, activities that make life complete. Yet, a person
may be free in this sense without being free in a deeper sense. He
may be free from the bonds of utility without being free from the
bonds of accepted opinions, particularly about the goodness of the
ends he pursues. Liberal education therefore strives to liberate the
young from the shackles of such opinions and from the bonds of
conventional views that pass for the truth of things, by teaching
them to reflect on ends, goods, and purposes. It is a radical inquiry
into ends.[29]

Liberal education aims to prepare young people for an intelligent life. Its most important goal is to teach them to become
thoughtful about themselves and the world, about their actions
and their thoughts, about what they do, what they say, what they
want, and what they think. It seeks to illuminate life, and particularly to clarify the fundamental human alternatives, by delving
as deeply as possible into the roots of things. Liberal education is
thus essentially a recovery or rediscovery of root issues and origins. As Eva Brann has argued, it aims at originality, not in the
familiar and futile sense of urging students to think something
new, but in the deeper and more rewarding sense of teaching them
to think things anew, to discover truths for themselves, not for the
world, to think things through to their true beginnings.[30] Liberal
education is thus chiefly the careful study of originating books or
texts—the seminal works of our intellectual tradition, which, by
establishing, clarifying, repudiating, reviving, and even seeking to
end that tradition, give us the greatest access to the root questions
and fundamental alternatives in life.

Let me explain what this suggestion means by contrasting it to
typical current policies and practices. It is often said nowadays
that science students should be required to take humanities

courses and humanities students should have to take science courses. The idea is of course to cover the ground of the intellectual globe by employing area or "group" distribution requirements, which emphasize the distance or polarity between different subjects. Given the fact that students today, regardless of whether they are science or humanities majors, tend to be very narrow, such cultural exchange requirements seem quite plausible at first. But what do students really gain from them? Do they become more thoughtful about their activities and serious concerns? Do such requirements do more than balance narrow technical competence with mere exposure and superficial breadth?

It is more important, it seems to me, for students to study more deeply in their own areas than to dabble in remote ones. By studying more deeply, I do not mean taking a greater number of advanced technical courses. Nor do I mean sacrificing breadth. I mean studying the authors whose thought brings to light the intellectual presuppositions of the student's specialized field. Physics students, for example, should study Aristotle, Bacon, Galileo, Descartes, Newton, Einstein, and other such authors. They should thoughtfully and rigorously pursue such quesitons as, What is science? What does the modern scientific method imply or presuppose about the world, about reason, about the possibility of knowing? What is time? What is space? What are mass, energy, and force? Similarly, students majoring in literature should study Plato, Aristotle, Locke, Hume, Kant, and Nietzsche, among others. They should pursue such questions as, What is the relation of language to thought? of form to meaning? of imagination to reason? of poetry to truth? What is reading? What is speech? What is literature? Every course of study should carefully reflect on its own conditions. Each discipline should examine the usually overlooked presuppositions governing the way in which it presents and examines its subjects as well as the presuppositions establishing it as a separate field. For example, what are "mathematical objects"? Do mathematical symbols constitute a language? And why has mathematics, once a liberal art, become separated from and even opposed to the humanities? Every discipline, reflecting on its own foundations, should ultimately pursue such questions as, What is learning? What is knowledge? What is truth?[31]

This liberal education is crucial to our universities, which are primarily concerned with the "ways of using reason" rather than with "the way of reason,"[32] in other words, with the knowledge of means rather than with the knowledge of ends. Such an education is also conducive to or improves upon the goals of both specialization and general education. It concentrates without narrowing and at the same time expands without diluting. Breadth becomes a consequence of, not a substitute for, intellectual rigor.

Yet, while such a liberal education belongs in the modern American university, it is not naturally at home there. Unlike general education, it cannot be simply grafted onto the university's departmental structure or assembled out of its parts. The emphasis on authors rather than on areas partly obviates the difficulty as it helps to avoid the problematical prejudgments underlying the division of knowledge and allows students (and faculty) a more natural pursuit of the basic questions. But liberal education faces a number of well-entrenched academic prejudices stemming from the artificial separation of science and the humanities. Philosophy, once considered the queen of the sciences, is now thought to be merely one of the many equal specialties; reason, once considered the highest authority in human life, has been largely banished from the humanities and confined to the natural sciences, which have arrogated to themselves the name of knowledge simply (*scientia*); and the humanities, in a rear-guard action to defend themselves from the destructive onslaughts on the sciences, have cut themselves off from nature, denying both the existence of the good and our capacity to know it by reason.

If liberal education is not naturally at home in the university, the university must establish and maintain a special place for it. I have in mind the sort of teaching programs that are sometimes called Honors or Liberal Studies programs. The great difficulty with such programs is that they are unavoidably dependent on departments, which usually have their own interests and priorities and often have different notions of what constitutes good teaching.

Moreover, the faculty's departmental affiliations produce for them a major conflict concerning research, which has a significant effect on teaching. The conflict involves the kind, not the volume, of research. Departments require their faculty to be productive scholars. This requirement is perfectly appropriate if "productive" means active. Too often, however, it takes on another connotation. I do not mean the familiar emphasis on the sheer number of publications or on the sort of research that can attract outside funding. I mean, instead, an emphasis on newness in areas in which scholarship is not a cumulative and corporate enterprise. In this emphasis, as in so many other respects, the humanities seem to ape the natural sciences. In the natural sciences, as previously discussed, knowledge is clearly progressive. New truths do not so much refute as build upon old ones. Discoveries are made, in Newton's words, by "standing on the shoulders of giants."[33] In the humanities, however, knowledge proceeds quite differently and perhaps even in a contrary manner. "In arts mechanical the first deviser comes shortest, and time addeth and perfecteth," writes Bacon; "but in sciences [by which he means "the philosophies and sciences of Aristotle, Plato," and other ancients] the first author goeth furthest, and time lesseth and corrupteth."[34] In the humanities the original insight may be the most profound, all subsequent understanding suffering from the perhaps unavoidable sedimentation that affects such knowledge.[35] "The possibility must be contemplated that in philosophy a pejorative principle is at work, that the loss of innocence, of immediacy, of naivete, must in the very nature of the thing bring with it a loss of depth."[36] This is why liberal education has no relation to the newness or the oldness of knowledge. Nevertheless, to be a "productive" scholar usually means to make a new or original contribution to one's field. And in fields where such contributions cannot really be expected, this demand becomes the peculiar if pervasive academic obligation to devote one's time and thought to a complete mastery of and contribution to the current secondary literature in one's field. Professors, no longer concerned with either the knowledge of means or the knowledge of ends, write books and articles about the books and articles written by other professors and hope that other professors will write books and articles about theirs. Thus research, far from being original in any sense of the term, becomes largely transformed into an ever-expanding network of secondary references. As "the advancement of learning" degenerates into merely keeping up with the latest trends and fashions in one's field, the humanities, after first being turned into a kind of dry scholasticism, finally lose their *raison d'etre*. They soon become the handmaids of convention, serving to bind young minds to rather than liberate them from the reigning intellectual orthodoxies of the day.

I believe that liberal education, properly understood, should be a vital part of the modern American university precisely because it offers a different kind of knowledge and has a different set of concerns from the university as a whole. As a rational search for ends, it is a necessary grounding—literally, an "understanding"—for what the rest of the university offers. Without liberal education, the university can do its major job of advancing and transmitting the sort of knowledge that leads to practical results, but it cannot do it well. On the contrary, liberal education makes university research truly "practical" by making the purposes for practice known. The German poet Schiller once observed that modern times are characterized by abstract science on the one side and unrefined passion on the other and there is nothing to connect and temper the two extremes. Much the same might be said of the American university. Reason is largely confined to abstract science and instrumental pursuits, and the greatest questions of life are left to purely personal passion and taste. The greatest challenge to the university in the years ahead is not whether it can continue to augment the storehouse of human knowledge, but whether it can teach men and women to use that knowledge to conduct their lives thoughtfully and well.

NOTES

1. Charles W. Eliot, *Educational Reform* (New York: The Century Co., 1898), p. 231.

2. Herbert Butterfield, *The Universities and Education Today* (London: Routledge & Kegan Paul Ltd., 1962), p. 19.

3. Alfred North Whitehead, *The Aims of Education and Other Essays* (New York: The Free Press, 1967), pp. 97-98.

4. *Nation*, 28 January 1875. Quoted in Abraham Flexner, *Daniel Coit Gilman*, (New York: Harcourt, Brace and Co., 1946), p. 50.

5. Abraham Flexner, *Universities—American, English, and German*, (New York: Oxford University Press, 1930), pp. 27-28.

6. Robert M. Hutchins, *No Friendly Voice* (Chicago: University of Chicago Press, 1936), p. 175.

7. The Carnegie Foundation for the Advancement of Teaching, *Second Annual Report*, (New York: 1907), p. 95.

8. "The Yale Report of 1828," in *The Colleges and the Public 1787-1862*, ed. Theodore Rawson Crane, Classics in Education Series No. 15 (New York: Bureau of Publications, Teachers College, 1963), p. 89; italics original.

9. "Francis Wayland's Report to the Corporation of Brown University, 1850," in *American Higher Education: A Documentary History*, ed. Richard Hofstadter and Wilson Smith (Chicago: University of Chicago Press, 1961), Vol. 2, pp. 482, 478.

10. Walter P. Rogers, *Andres D. White and the Modern University* (Ithaca, N.Y.: Cornell University Press, 1942), p. 47.

11. Alexis de Tocqueville, *Democracy in America*, Vol. II, bk. 1, x.

12. Hofstadter and Smith, *Documentary History*, Vol. 1, pp. 482-483.

13. Thomas Jefferson, "Report of the Rockfish Gap Commission on the Proposed University of Virginia, 1818," ibid., Vol. 1, p. 196; italics original.

14. *Johns Hopkins University: Twenty-fifth Anniversary* (Baltimore: The Johns Hopkins Press, 1902), pp. 59, 39.

15. Laurence R. Veysey, *The Emergence of the American University*, (Chicago: University of Chicago Press, 1965), p. 144.

16. "Henry P. Tappan on the Idea of the True University, 1858," in Hofstadter and Smith, *Documentary History*, Vol. 2, p. 528.

17. Descartes, *Discourse on Method*, Part 2.

18. Harry D. Gideonse, *The Higher Learning in a Democracy: A Reply*

President Hutchins' Critique of the American University (New York: Farrar and Rinehardt, 1937), p. 19. The reference is to Flexner, *Universities*, p. 23.

19. Gideonse, *Reply to Hutchins*, p. 24.

20. Ibid., p. 18. The references are to Robert M. Hutchins, *The Higher Learning in America* (New Haven, Conn.: Yale University Press, 1936), p. 59; and Flexner, *Universities*, pp. 17-18.

21. Thomas Hobbes, *Leviathan*, ch. 5.

22. Gideonse, *Reply to Hutchins*, p. 28.

23. Fragment 40, Diels.

24. Allan Bloom, "The Crisis of Liberal Education," in *Higher Education and Modern Democracy*, ed. Robert A. Goldwin (Chicago: Rand McNally and Co., 1967), p. 130.

25. Two influential if somewhat opposite examples of the confusion between liberal and general education are the 1945 Harvard Report on General Education and *The Reforming of General Education* by Daniel Bell. Writing in the Introduction to the Harvard Report, James B. Conant states that "The heart of the problem of a general education is the continuance of the liberal and humane tradition," adding that "today, we are concerned with a general education—a liberal education—not for the relatively few, but for a multitude." *General Education in a Free Society: Report of the Harvard Committee* (Cambridge, Mass.: Harvard University Press, 1945), p. viii. President Conant explains that the only reason the term "general" rather than "liberal" appears in the report's title has to do with certain considerations concerning its intended audience, and not with anything concerning the substance or the character of the education it discusses (ibid., p. ix). Bell follows the Harvard Report by using the terms "general education" and "liberal education" synonymously at the same time that he rejects its major premise by collapsing the distinction between general and specialized education on the grounds of the supremacy of method over substance. See *The Reforming of General Education: The Columbia College Experience in its National Setting* (New York: Columbia University Press, 1966), e.g., p. 8.

26. Eva T. H. Brann, *Paradoxes of Education in a Republic* (Chicago: University of Chicago Press, 1979), p. 60.

27. *Politics*, VII, 1333a-b.

28. Ibid., VIII, 1337b.

29. Brann, *Paradoxes*, pp. 61-63; Jacob Klein, "On Liberal Education," (Lecture delivered at St. Mary's College, California, 25 March 1965;

Annapolis, Md.: St. John's College Press, 1965), p. 1; Mark Van Doren, *Liberal Education* (New York: Henry Holt and Co., 1943), ch. 4; Leo Strauss, "Liberal Education and Responsibility," in *Liberalism: Ancient and Modern* (New York: Basic Books, 1968); Allan Bloom, "The Crisis of Liberal Education"; and Charles Wegener, *Liberal Education and the Modern University* (Chicago: University of Chicago Press, 1978), ch. 4.

30. Brann, *Paradoxes*, pp. 102-119.

31. On natural science in a liberal arts curriculum, see Joseph J. Schwab, "The Nature of Scientific Knowledge as Related to Liberal Education," in *Science, Curriculum, and Liberal Education* (Chicago: University of Chicago Press, 1978).

32. Brann, *Paradoxes*, p. 121

33. Letter to Hooke, 5 February 1675/6.

34. Francis Bacon, *The Advancement of Learning*, I. iv. 12.

35. For the problem of "sedimentation," see Edmund Husserl, *The Crisis of European Sciences* (Evanston, Ill.: Northwestern University Press, 1970) and "Philosophy as a Rigorous Science" in *Husserl: Shorter Works* (Notre Dame, Ind.: University of Notre Dame Press, 1981); and Jacob Klein, "Phenomenology and the History of Science" in *Philosophical Essays in Memory of Edmund Husserl*, ed. Marvin Farber (Cambridge, Mass.: Harvard University Press, 1940), pp. 143-163.

36. Brann, *Paradoxes*, p. 113.

Frank B. Murray

Paradoxes of a University at Risk

In the spring of 1983, the secretary of education's National Commission on Excellence in Education, after eighteen months of study, reported that due to a rising tide of mediocrity the quality of American schooling had eroded over the last two decades to a point that threatened the very future of the nation and its people. The nation, the commission concluded, was at risk, and so, by implication, was the American college and university; not just because the students in the colleges and universities were so recently students in the afflicted high schools, but because the same rising tide was also at the university and college doors. The same forces that could be said to have eroded the public schools operated as well in the institutions of higher education. As we shall see, the lessons from the 1983 reports on the quality of elementary and secondary education are virtually the same for colleges and high schools.

Throughout the year scores of reports by other blue-ribbon commissions and task forces sought to confirm the thesis that once again the nation's failures in the world marketplace and in diplomacy could be attributed to the failure of the nation's common schools to produce children who have mastered certain critical skills. With a remarkable sameness, the authors of 12 major national reports and nearly 150 state-level reports echoed the findings of the National Commmission on Excellence and called for the same set of educational reforms: more time devoted to the study of basic core disciplines and more rigorous assessment of the academic achievements of students and their teachers.

None of the commissions called for a radical reform of the public schools or an abandonmet of them to other promising ways of education—as well they might, given their pessimistic evaluations of the public schools' accomplishments. Instead, the nation's commitment to universal public schooling, perhaps the unique American contribution to civilization, was as firm in these reports as its faith that education was still the way to transform both the child and the nation. The salvation of the nation was in its schools; education, the American secular religion, was still, as a September 1982 Gallup poll indicated, the best guarantee of a strong America for 84 percent of the respondents (compared to a second place 66 percent for industry or 47 percent third place for the military). The nation's annual financial commitment to education, a staggering $230 billion, approximately $3,300 per pupil in elementary and secondary education, was to be increased, not reduced, in light of education's failures. One of every four Americans would remain either a student or employee in the educational system, and each commission or task force, one way or another, called for an increase in the allocation of people—particularly talented people—to this enormous educational enterprise.

The Commission on Excellence in Education, along with the other national groups, attempted to support their analyses with several lines of evidence that, if trustworthy, could have led the commissioners to reject the traditional faith that the schools can effect any substantial change in the country's future, particularly its economic future. There is a paradox, one of many, in their analysis of the school's shortcomings as a crisis of major proportion and their proposed remedies of a mere bureaucratic tightening of the school's operation. There is also the paradox of the effects of schooling on the national economy: on the one hand, there are estimates that up to one-half the increase in the gross national

product over the last twenty years is due to the increased educational level of the work force,[1] but on the other hand, there is
almost no evidence that differences in educational attainment have
any bearing on differences in on-the-job productivity.[2] While education clearly helps people gain a desirable position, especially if
credentials are required for it, it cannot be shown by our current
methods that education will help them do well in those positions.
If only because the present elementary and secondary schools will
prepare only ten percent of the labor force of the 1990s, we would
not expect, as the commissioners do, that even full acceptance of
their recommendations could have much impact on the economy.
Apart from the fact that common recommendations—more time,
more work—may have no chance to improve the schools,[3] there is
apparently little chance that modifications in the public schools
will influence significantly the nation's immediate economic position either.

More remarkable still is the fact that these reports, which were
admittedly political polemics that went well beyond the data, were
so widely believed that the quality of education in the nation's
fifteen thousand school districts became a political issue at the national level. Even though opinion polls repeatedly find that the
public is more satisfied with local schools, of which they have
some knowledge, than they are with schools in general, there has
been a steady and undeniable erosion in the public's confidence in
their schools. This erosion, which began in the 1960s, is part of a
pervasive lack of confidence in all societal institutions.[4] There is
simply a well-founded distrust of the capacity and wisdom of the
leaders of our governments, armies, churches, businesses, unions,
schools, and so on to guide the nation. Still, the National Opinion
Surveys on public confidence show that education places third—
behind medicine and science—among the institutions in which people still have a great deal of confidence.[5] Nevertheless, the question
of why some members of the public were so receptive to the allega-
tions in the reports, and why some were outraged, bears further
examination. The answer, in part, lies in another paradox, one
explicitly stated (although not highlighted) in the excellence com-

mission report. While the average citizen is undeniably better educated, more knowledgeable, and more literate than the average citizen of twenty-five to thirty years ago, the averge high school graduate is not as well-educated as his far less numerous counterpart of three decades ago. These statements about the average citizen and the average graduate are both true, and it is not possible to comprehend the national debate on educational quality without confronting the fact of the truth of each statement.

The matter is complicated by several inherent tensions in the American educational system or lack of system (e.g., no reference to education is made in the United States Constitution). For whose benefit is the enterprise conducted: the pupil's, the parent's, the taxpayer's, the state's? What is the point of schooling: economic growth, mastery of subject matter, realization of the pupil's developmental potentials, and so on? The answer to these questions, historically, has been a function of the nation's prosperity and security. In times during which the nation's economy and security are threatened, the mission of the schools shifts and becomes narrowly focused upon the mastery of basic skills that are thought to be the foundation for a technological advantage over our competitors in the world markets and in spheres of diplomatic and military influence. In more tranquil times, the mission of the schools expands to encompass more humanitarian objectives, and the focus is on the pupil's well-being and development. It is not that these are mutually exclusive goals, although they can be, but that the measures of accountability shift from one period to another. Thus, the basis of an educational crisis may be only the crisis-maker's measurement of tasks that the school had not set for itself—or had not emphasized.

On the whole the schools succeed at what they attempt, at what they devote their resources to; and their failures rest mostly on taking wrong missions, or at least unenlightened ones. As Gary Sykes and others point out, the schools—for quite understandable reasons—often strike a deal or a bargain with some of their students, the essence of which is: "You leave me alone and I'll leave you alone and together we'll get through this compulsory schooling thing with the minimum stress and effort for both of us."[6] Thus, the "deal" becomes the mission in this instance, and the deal is what is learned and probably learned well. Similarly, as Theodore Sizer observes, even the very best teachers working in ideal conditions compromise at every turn.[7] For example, they cannot possibly read all the papers they know they should assign, so they assign fewer. They cannot possibly give each assigned paper the attention it deserves, so they don't; and so on, as one compromise after another is made in sound educational practice. Whatever the publicly endorsed mission or curriculum of the schools, there is the actual, sometimes hidden, curriculum of the schools—the deals and compromises—the bureaucratic consequences of compelling large numbers of children to attend school. The case for the effectiveness of the school, good or poor as that case is, must be placed in the context of the actual, the hidden, curriculum. The evidence of a national crisis must be taken in the same context—the inevitable consequences of attempting to manage and educate relatively large groups of children and adolescents.

The Evidence of Crisis

Whether "deals" or "compromises" were struck in the past, as certainly they were, or whether they are made more often now than in the past is not as important a question as whether there is an educational crisis. In fact, has the nation ever not been at risk? Have the schools ever achieved what their advocates hoped they would? Has any generation met, let alone exceeded, the prior generation's hopes for it? What evidence could there possibly be for a crisis, and was that evidence available in 1983, the year of the reports? And most important of all, how will we know when the crisis is over, i.e., when the nation is no longer at risk?

The National Commission on Excellence in Education cited thirteen representative indicators of risk: one contrasted pupils' achievement in the United States with the higher achievement of elite pupils in other countries, five characterized low levels of current academic proficiency in America, and seven showed that some measures of academic achievement had declined over the last twenty years. Part of the problem with these indicators, and any set for that matter, is that the country has very little reliable information about the quality of education and the factors that shape it.[8] It is no surprise that the data presented by most of the commissions, when viewed critically, are better evidence of the poverty of educational data and analysis than they are of the state of education.[9] Almost none of the evidence presented meets the ordinary tests for a scholarly review or interpretation of the research literature and, in several instances, the commissioners ignored the data and analyses prepared for them by their consultants. For example, in a background paper for the Twentieth Century Final Report, Making the Grade, Peterson concluded that "nothing in these data permits the conclusion that educational institutions have deteriorated badly."[10] As Buttercup noted in H.M.S. Pinafore, "Things are seldom what they seem, skim milk masquerades as cream."

The evidence from national assessments of academic achievement is complicated because, while some standardized tests scores have declined, others have remained stable and some have increased.[11] Delaware's Task Force, for example, came to the same conclusions and recommendations as the other groups, despite the fact that school children's performance on the California Achievement Test, the test by which Delaware assesses itself, has steadily increased and is, at every grade level, above the performance of the normative sample upon which the test was standardized. Moreover, despite the fact that these positive outcomes were reported in the press, opinion polls showed that the public was largely unaware of them and, in fact, tended to believe that school performance had deteriorated.[12] Some of the debate on test scores rests on the comical aspiration that everyone be above average, but most of it rests upon the naive assumption that the tests truly measure something that occurs in the schools—or perhaps something that should have occurred in the schools.

It is not possible for most standardized tests to measure adequately the pupil's acquisition of the curriculum, because the tests must be fair to the several textbook series that are widely used in the schools. Seventy-five percent of the schools, in fact, use one or another of four textbook series, and the content of the common achievement tests matches the content of these series only 30 to 40 percent of the time. The degree of overlap between curricular and test content is an ongoing problem for educational evaluators, particularly in times like the last two decades when the content of the curriculum has shifted markedly. It is, of course, difficult to know whether the pupils are mastering certain portions of the curriculum when large portions of it are not measured. Often the most interesting aspects of pupils' achievement are not measured because these achievements do not lend themselves to measurement in the common standardized test formats.

More perplexing than our inability to measure convincingly what transpires in the schools is the national fixation with test results that are not by any criterion a measure of the schools' effectiveness. Virtually every national report cites the six percent decline in Scholastic Aptitude Test (SAT) scores between 1963 and 1982 as a significant indicator, often the most powerful indicator, of the grave decline in the quality of schooling. Much of the public's ready acceptance of the bad news in the 1983 reports was conditioned, no doubt, by Educational Testing Service's announcement in 1966, and every year thereafter until 1982, that national SAT scores were lower than they were in previous years. Yet no responsible person argues that the SAT, by design or otherwise, measures the student's mastery of the curriculum or the school's effectiveness in teaching it. What then does the SAT measure and—if it is an important thing—to what can the decline in scores be attributed?

Apart from measuring how well students perform on other standardized tests, the SAT is designed to measure, or predict, how well a young person will perform in the college curriculum. Even here, students' SAT performance accounts for only 9 percent of the variability in their college grades; the other 91 percent of the variability is explained by other factors, the most significant of which is their record of achievement in high school. The SAT measures success in college, but not very well; yet the crisis in education is largely defined in terms of declining SAT scores. Moreover, and incredibly, the end of the crisis will be seen in terms of a rise in these scores to pre-1965 levels.[13]

The facts of the decline are, more or less, as follows: Between 1952 and 1963, at a time when the percentage of high school seniors taking the test rose from 6.8 percent to 50 percent—or from 81,000 to 933,000 students—the scores fluctuated randomly from year to year. Between 1963 and 1982, the scores fell 90 points (55 points verbal and 35 points math out of 800 points on each test); this represents a drop in about seven actual items from the verbal test and four items from the mathematics test. It was not the case that the tests became harder; if anything, they became easier (e.g., 3,000 students from 66 schools who took both the 1963 and 1973 versions scored from 8 to 12 points higher on the later version). It was the case that about half the total drop, and almost all the drop between 1960 and 1970, can be explained by changes in the composition of the group who took the tests. During the 1960s, for example, proportionately more students with lower scores aspired to college and took the test, and a small number of would-be high scorers elected not to attend college and therefore did not take the test.[14]

The declines after 1970, about 50 points, are more difficult to explain because they happened in all types of schools (private, public, large, small, high and low socioeconomic neighborhoods) and to all kinds of people—men, women, whites, blacks, and vale-dictorians. Indeed, by 1976, there were about 80,000 fewer students who scored above 600 on either the math or verbal tests than there were in 1970.

There exist at least fifty plausible theories about the causes of the decline, no one of which adequately accounts for more than a few points of the decrease in performance.[15] Felson and Land were even able to describe the entire SAT decline as well as the recent upturn with a model based solely upon demographic changes, without regard to any educational or school factors whatsoever.[16] Of course, it is reasonable to suppose that changes in the schools—absenteeism, grade inflation, reduction of homework to three hours per week, and proliferation of electives—could be correlated with students' performance on these national tests. Although the quality of new entrants to the teaching profession is low by traditional academic measures, lower than in the recent past, it is not reasonable to attribute the SAT decline to their presence in the system. In the first place, there were relatively few of them; and in the second place, the decline in SAT scores among teacher education students, while sharper than students in general, coincided with the general decline of everyone's scores.

The decline in SAT scores has been accompanied, paradoxically, by an equally dramatic increase in high school grades.[17] In the 1960s, there were twice as many students in high school with C averages as A averages; now there are the same number of each. To their credit, a clear majority of entering freshmen say that grading in high school was too lenient. While there are several explanations for the phenomenon of higher grades but lower SAT scores, the issue of the school's tangible accomplishments, whatever they are, is paramount.

The School's Accomplishments

It is clear that schooling occurs in a larger context of pervasive forces that significantly dampen, perhaps on occasion facilitate, the effects schools can have.[18] On the whole, educational researchers have great difficulty demonstrating unambiguously the effects of schooling—either because the effects, as the critics maintain, are minuscule or negative, or because the effects are swamped by other factors—factors that by comparison exert enormous influence on the intellectual development of the child and that, by and large, are not under the control of the schools.

It is still another paradox of the 1983 report debate that while we hold the schools responsible for our diminished position in the international community, we are able to find so few clear and unambiguous effects of schooling on any individual's later success or failure. This is not to say that schooling does not have effects; on the contrary, the point is that schools on the whole affect that which they try to affect, but the effects are limited generally to the specific and immediate context in which they take place. The notable successes of the contemporary schools, for example, are the gains in minority achievement, an area that was the target of several recent federal and state educational programs. In fact, the recent upturn in SAT scores is entirely attributable to gains in the performance of minority students. Similarly, the National Assessment of Educational Progress (NAEP) showed significant gains between 1975 and 1980 in basic arithmetical skills and in reading— both areas that were targeted for attention in the 1970s. At the same time, there were disturbing declines on NAEP scores in science and mathematical problem solving—areas that may have been slighted in the recent back-to-basics movements.[19] Project Head Start, a deliberate and expensive effort ($6,000 per child) to alter the typical academic careers of disadvantaged children can claim the following effects: the Head Start pupils eventually led their counterparts by a grade level in reading and mathematics, had half their juvenile delinquency rate, and had half their special education placement rate.[20]

When school achievement is viewed from a cumulative perspective, as a set of consistent increments in what the pupil knows and can do, the picture is one of a steady upward growth curve, particularly strong in the early grades with a uniform and somewhat puzzling slowdown in the later grades, but continual growth nevertheless. When children are withdrawn from school for significant periods of time—more than a year—there are serious, sometimes irreversible, regressions in their intellectual abilities and academic proficiency.[21] Similarly, the inevitable declines in intelligence test performance by older adults is postponed for those who attend school for significant numbers of years.[22]

Those who wish to take the national standardized test score data as clear evidence for a serious erosion of the quality of American education must also confront evidence from several independent sources that while some of these scores have decreased in varying amounts, others have increased; that student populations have changed as the power of the high schools to retain students (now about 80 percent) grew to encompass lower-ability students who in an earlier time would have dropped out of school (50 percent in 1950); that curricula and tests change, not always in a synchronous way; and that the methodology of the behavioral sciences is sufficiently error-ridden so that dependable data are rare and valid data are even rarer. Finally, it must be understood that several critical concepts in the debate, literacy for instance, are not defined consistently nor well thought out theoretically. The prevalence of illiteracy in the country is a significant issue, but one that is poorly served, for instance, by the Excellence Commission's simple assertion, often repeated, that 23 million American adults are functionally illiterate.[23] Apart from the fact that the study upon which the claim is made is flawed, careful analysis of the reading-trend data supports "the conclusion that today's children are better readers than children from any period in the past and that improvement in this area has been continuous in the history of education in the United States."[24] The point is that a convincing treatment of critical notions, like illiteracy or reading comprehension, has eluded even the best thinkers in the field.

The Link to Higher Education

Even when large portions of the commission and task-force conclusions are discounted in recognition of their reliance on poor data and superficial analysis, their conclusions are sobering. Although the quality of American education may not be as uniformly bad as the reports indicate, one is hard pressed to find evidence that it is uniformly good—or that it ever was. The fact is that, as was noted earlier, today's high school graduate, despite his higher grades, is not as educationally accomplished as his counterpart of a generation ago. Moreover, there is a sharp and continuing decrease in popularity for virtually every field that has a basis in the liberal arts.[25]

Yet in 1984 when the American Council on Education surveyed 486 institutions with undergraduate programs and 383 with graduate programs, it found that 60 percent reported no significant change in the quality of their students, graduate or undergraduate, who were majoring in science and engineering. In fact, about 25 percent reported that the quality of students had improved over the last five years. Faculty members, while they may complain about their students' lack of academic aptitude and commitment, have tended, nevertheless, to give them the same grades—actually somewhat higher grades—than they gave their predecessors. At the same time, colleges and universities across the country are having to commit increasing resources to remedial programs for their students.

The public's confidence in higher education, while still relatively high—second only to medicine—has also eroded steadily from 1966 onward.[25] It is destined to erode further as it will be found that all the criticisms leveled against the high schools in 1983 can be leveled—with equal legitimacy—against the institutions of higher education.[27] Since 1965, for example, the decline in Graduate Record Examination (GRE) scores has exceeded the SAT declines. Of course, the same cautions addressed earlier in the interpretation of the SAT decline apply to whatever interpretations are given to the GRE decline. It should be noted that the GRE is scaled to the performance of 2,095 students who took the test in 1952 and were not representative of any population. They cannot be said to be representative of all college graduates nor of all graduate school applicants. Thus, the interpretation of the scores, absolutely or relatively, is limited.

While the scores for the College Board achievement tests, taken by high school seniors, have been stable—even increasing in some areas—scores on the GRE achievement tests, taken by college seniors, have declined approximately 15 percent in English and history, for example. Put simply, like the high school diploma, "the college degree is no longer a reliable indicator of competence."[28] Based upon this line of reasoning, we have every reason to expect colleges and universities to be charged with the same deficiencies attributed to high schools.

Even in this disturbing turn of events, there is the paradox of the palpable indicators of declining student performance (each with its limitations, to be sure) coupled with equally powerful indicators of increased tangible intellectual accomplishment. There are, for example, clear signs of a downward migration of curriculum content throughout all levels of the educational system. Calculus, once exclusively taken by college freshmen or sophomores, is now routinely studied by high school seniors. Reading, once taught in the first grade, is now regularly introduced in the kindergarten. Adults frequently report that experiences and concepts that came late in their development are encountered or mastered at much earlier ages by the rising generation. The generation gaps in the acquisition of new skills, like those in computing science, indicate that the younger generations do not lack the capacity to adapt successfully to a rapidly altered society. Law School Admission Test (LSAT) scores and Medical College Admission Test (MCAT) scores have increased, for example, and there are any number of examples of young peoples' competence in all professions and occupations, some of which did not exist a few years ago.

It is a remarkable occurrence that the nation has so little information about the academic achievement and performance of college students. There has not been a National Assessment of Educational Progress at the higher education levels, but despite the appalling lack of systematic and comprehensive measurement of the academic progress of college students, there is some evidence that colleges and universities are effective in this regard. Students, naturally enough, can be shown—on the basis of Graduate Record Examination (GRE) achievement tests—to know best what they majored in, and seniors know more—a full standard deviation more—than juniors.[29]

Similarly, it can be shown that college graduates, across several ages and time periods, know more than high school graduates, who in turn know more than elementary school graduates, about the kind of topical information contained in national surveys. Education, particularly at college and university levels, has large, pervasive, and enduring effects on what we know and how receptive we are to new information.

Some Consequences of Educational Expansion

Whatever specific educational missions the American public schools have proclaimed at various times, the overriding and uniquely American mission was the extension of schooling to all children, even if it meant simply compelling more and more children to go to school for longer and longer periods.[30] In 1970, only 37 percent of children attended preschool and kindergarten; now nearly double that percentage attend. At the turn of the century, only 10 percent of the nation's fourteen- to seventeen-year-olds attended high school, and now 94 percent attend. In 1950, 55 percent of white students and 30 percent of black students graduated from high school, and today 85 percent and 75 percent respectively of white and black students graduate from high school. Approximately 70 percent of the graduates go on to college and, of those, 50 percent earn a college degree. The pressure to extend college education to all citizens is manifest in sharp increases in college enrollments—from three million in 1960 to over twelve million now—and in the phenomenal growth of the junior and community colleges, with nearly one new institution opening each week throughout the 1960s. This pressure will continue, and it inevitably places at risk the traditional role of the college or university as an institution that sorts out people for the various professions and gives it another time-honored role, that of assisting each person to fully use his or her intellectual potential. "When everyone is somebody," concluded Gilbert and Sullivan in the *Gondoliers*, "then no one's anybody."

The establishment of universal schooling carries with it the risk, as Torsten Husén observed, of the installation of a new underclass, those who from the very beginning of their schooling are failures.[31] Education, far from equalizing opportunity, exacerbates and creates differences in levels of mastery of competencies needed in our technologically based society. A comprehensive review of educational research demonstrates a striking, but perhaps not surprising, phenomenon: the beneficial growth during educational or other experiences is such that those who score higher on pretests,

or have other desirable and appropriate attributes, gain absolutely and disproportionately more than do others who share the same
experience.[32] The phenomenon is sometimes called the "fan-
spread" effect because the increasing variation between people during the course of a treatment leads to a fan-spread of data points
when achievement is plotted against time. Sometimes the effect is
referred to as the "Matthew" effect after the Apostle Matthew,
who wrote, "For the man who has will always be given more, till
he has enough and to spare; and the man who has not will forfeit
even the little he has" (Matthew 25:29).

The creation of a new underclass, like the poor who get poorer,
is the most serious educational problem facing us, and yet this
group has been overlooked in all the national reports. Like the
poor who are always with us, the potential for a new underclass in
higher education is good; the signs of it exist in the pressure for
open admission and costly remediation, in the redundancy in curricula at all levels, in the proliferation of incoherent occupational
degrees and specialties, and in entrepreneurial and proprietary
ventures that diffuse the point of higher education.

The top four to nine percent of students in industrialized nations throughout the world from comprehensive and selective high
schools are comparable, for example, in their mastery of science
and mathematics.[33] The concern for them in the national reports is
misplaced in this regard, and the salient educational reform recommendations addressed to them are likely to increase drop-out
rates of the others, already on the rise, and increase the spread
further in the levels of educated intelligence.

The sheer magnitude of the universal schooling enterprise also
carries with it the requirement that the educational enterprise—at
all levels—be operated by large numbers of relatively untalented
persons. There simply are not enough people in the country between the ages of twenty-one and seventy who score at the top
end of any credible test of intellectual competence to fill three
million teaching positions and to do the other complicated work of
the nation. As a result, the nation, of necessity, has had to design
an educational system—at all levels—which persons from the

lower ends of the talent distribution can operate with tolerable levels of success. Throughout the nation's history and as an implicit tenet of public policy, we have held to the proposition that only small portions of the available population of highly talented persons should be allocated to work in the public schools. In fact, the best interests of the nation are thought to be served if the best and the brightest generally work in other places.

While the decline in the academic competence of prospective teachers is well-documented and widely known, it is not widely appreciated that colleges and universities may be exposed to the same condition and risk as GRE scores decline and as the economic competition for talent shifts further to the advantage of industry and the military. Computer science departments, for example, can rarely afford to hire their own graduates. The percentage of college students who plan to pursue careers in college teaching has declined from 3.4 percent in 1966 to 0.2 percent in 1981. When the large number of faculty who entered the profession in the 1960s retire together in 15 or so years, their likely replacements will long since have taken up other lines of work. The future scarcity of people with Ph.D.s, coupled with demands for admission to higher education by the baby-boom generation's offspring, will replicate closely the conditions currently faced by the public schools as they scramble to attract talented people to careers in teaching.

In summary, the lessons from the various 1983 reports on the quality of education are largely the same for high schools and colleges. That our colleges and universities have not noticed this fact indicates that the risk to higher education is greater than it needs to be. The evidence of risks and the imperatives for reform cited by the National Commission on Excellence in Education apply with equal force across the continuum of schooling. The notion that high school and college are qualitatively distinct and unique activities will not serve the colleges well as they struggle with the same issues that preoccupied, or should have preoccupied, the glittering array of national talent on the national panels on excellence in education. In part, the issues come down to technical matters of how to engineer effective schools, schools that produce excellence and simultaneously maximize the pupil's potential at all levels in the distribution of talent. As colleges take on the mission of the "effective college," as inevitably they must, they will reduce the risk of failure by a careful examination of the educational policies and practices that precede and follow the college years.

NOTES

1. C. W. Fowler, "Only Masochists Could Accept the Findings of the Excellence Commission," *The American School Board Journal* (September 1983), pp. 43-49.

2. V. Tinto, "Does Schooling Matter? A Retrospective Assessment," in *Review of Research in Education,* vol. 5, ed. Lee Shulman, (Itasca, Indiana: F. E. Peacock Publishers, 1977).

3. L. Stedman and M. Smith, "Recent Reform Proposals for American Education," *Contemporary Education Review* (in press).

4. A. Levine and D. Haselkorn, "For the Sake of the Children: The Demise of Educational Consensus in America," *National Forum* 64:2 (1984), pp. 5-11.

5. H. Hodgkinson, "What's Still Right with Education," *Phi Delta Kappan* (1982), pp. 231-235.

6. G. Sykes, "Teaching in America: The Deal," *The Wilson Quarterly/ New Year's 1984* (1984), pp. 59-77.

7. T. R. Sizer, *Horace's Compromise* (New York: Houghton-Mifflin Co., 1984).

8. G. Austin and H. Garber, *The Rise and Fall of National Test Scores* (New York: Academic Press, 1982).

9. Stedman and Smith, "Recent Reform Proposals."

10. P. E. Peterson, in Twentieth Century Task Force on Federal Elementary and Secondary Educational Policy, *Making the Grade* (New York: Twentieth Century Fund, 1983), p. 59.

11. Austin and Garber, *The Rise and Fall of National Test Scores;* H. Hodgkinson, "What's Right with Education," *Phi Delta Kappan* (1979), pp. 159-162; Fowler, "Only Masochists Could Accept the Findings."

12. J. Raffel, N. J. Colmer, and D. L. Berry, "Public Opinion Toward the Public Schools of Northern New Castle County," College of Urban Affairs and Public Policy (Newark, Delaware: University of Delaware, 9 May 1983).

13. See, for example, T. H. Bell, "American Education at the Cross-roads," *Phi Delta Kappan* (1984), pp. 531-534.

14. B. Eckland, "College Entrance Examination Trends," in G. Austin and H. Garber, *The Rise and Fall of National Test Scores* (New York: Academic Press, 1982).

15. Ibid.

16. M. Felson and K. Land, "Social, Demographic and Interrelationships with Educational Trends in the United States, 1947-1974," *Research in Population Economics* 1 (1982), pp. 93-125.

17. A. Astin, "Student Values: Knowing More About Where We Are Today," *Bulletin of the American Association for Higher Education* 36:9 (1984), pp. 10-13.

18. See, for example, J. Coleman, *Equality of Educational Opportunity* (Washington, D.C.: U.S. Government Printing Office, 1966).

19. R. Brown, "Public Policy and Pupil Achievement," *State Legislatures* (October 1983), pp. 39-41.

20. Hodgkinson, "What's Still Right with Education."

21. See, for example, Austin and Garber, *The Rise and Fall of National Test Scores.*

22. E. Brody and N. Brody, *Intelligence: Nature, Determinants, and Consequences* (New York: Academic Press, 1976).

23. Stedman and Smith, "Recent Reform Proposals," and R. Farr and L. Fay, "Reading Trend Data in the United States," in Austin and Garber, *The Rise and Fall of National Test Scores.*

24. Farr and Fay, "Reading Trend Data," p. 135.

25. Astin, "Student Values."

26. Levine and Haselkorn, "For the Sake of the Children."

27. C. Adelman, "Getting Up Off the Floor: Standards and Realities in Higher Education," *AGB Reports: The Journal of the Association of Governing Boards of Universities and Colleges* (July/August 1983), pp. 13-19.

28. Ibid., p. 17.

29. C. R. Pace, *Measuring Outcomes of College: Fifty Years of Findings and Recommendations for the Future* (San Francisco: Jossey-Bass, 1979).

30. J. E. Craig, "The Expansion of Education," in *Review of Research in Education,* vol. 9, ed. D. Berliner, (Itasca, Indiana: F. E. Peacock Publishers, 1981).

31. T. Huse¹n, "Are Standards in U.S. Schools Really Lagging Behind Those in Other Countries?" *Phi Delta Kappan* (1983), pp. 455-461.

32. H. Walberg and S. Tsai, "Matthew Effects in Education," *American*

Educational Research Journal 20 (1983), pp. 359-373.
    33. Husén, "Are Standards in U.S. Schools Really Lagging Behind?"

Eric Brucker

Managing the University
for Excellence

Countless commencement speakers admonish graduating college
students that they are about to enter the real world—as if the
college experience is, in some fundamental sense, "unreal" rather
than just different in kind. While there *are* significant differences
between the missions and management of not-for-profit and profit-
oriented organizations, there are also striking similarities. To the
extent that similarities exist, it follows that the management skills
and techniques used in America's best corporate organizations
might also be effective within a university environment.

I.

When business activity was directed predominately toward the
production of tangible output, the natural tendency was to view
institutions committed to producing intangibles such as knowledge
as being fundamentally different. When the primary motivation
for work within the business sector was immediate economic reward, it was also natural to emphasize the contrast with students
and faculty who were working to gain new knowledge and personal insight. Now, however, as our economy enters the postin-

dustrial age, business firms are becoming more like universities, with their most important activities becoming information- and knowledge-driven. Similarly, the motivations of business workers, university faculty, and students have grown more alike. Economic considerations are still an important motivator in business, but increased and broader importance is now assigned to the overall quality of the individual's environment, which permits personal growth and development.

While highlighting business-university similarities, we should not lose sight of the fact that universities are fundamentally different from profit-oriented firms in at least one important respect. Universities do not, cannot, and should not sell their products in markets where prices are primarily determined by the interaction of private demand and supply. The provision of new knowledge and the dissemination of existing knowledge cannot be sold in the market like the services or products of most corporations. Individuals surely do benefit personally from receiving an education—but so does society. Selling collegiate education as one might sell widgets or deodorant would ignore the existence of the many social benefits of education that go well beyond those directly realized by the individual. The true value to society of creating a knowledge-able citizenry, of the continuation of our cultural heritage, or of gaining new basic knowledge about our physical or social world cannot be priced and sold in any private market.

At the same time, too much has been made of the observation that profit-oriented institutions have a clear measure of success in the "bottom line" of the profit and loss statement, while universities do not. Universities do not have a simple bottom-line measure of success, but we should also recognize that the corporate "bottom line" is far from the precise measurement that some claim. At base, the ultimate social value of both profit and not-for-profit organizations rests upon external assessments of how well they perform in meeting society's needs in a creative and cost-effective way. Informed stockholders are fully aware of the danger of assessing the present and future value of a corporation solely by some "bottom-line" accounting measure. Accounting conventions designed to deal with a wide variety of tax and related issues certainly make the meaning of the corporate "bottom line" at least somewhat ambiguous.

Stockholder assessment of a company's ability to continuously create products and services that meet the needs of customers, rather than annual accounting profit, may be the best overall measure of long-term corporate success. Similarly, the long-term success of a university or college is determined by external groups. Alumni, legislators, foundations and individual donors, accreditation agencies, other peer groups, and present and future students are constantly evaluating the success of a university.

II.

Excessive focus on accounting and legal dissimilarities tends to obscure the many managerial similarities between business and institutions of higher education. Both types of organizations are ultimately evaluated by broader measures than a simple bottom-line accounting measure; individuals working in both types of organizations have similar personal needs and motivations, and both are affected by similar trends in societal values and aspirations.

As universities prepare to meet an increasingly uncertain future, valuable managerial insights can be gained by examining the management structure and style that characterize the best corporate organizations.

Many, if not most, of the observations made by Thomas Peters and Robert Waterman in their bestseller *In Search of Excellence: Lessons from America's Best-Run Companies* have direct significance for the management of America's universities.[1] Peters and Waterman start with the premise that successful organizations are not described well by using highly complex and rational models. Their deemphasis of Taylorism and the traditional rational conceptualization of the planning, organizing, and control functions of management is refreshing. Likewise, Anthony Athos and Richard Pascale in *The Art of Japanese Management* stress that traditional American management theory and practice may have placed excessive emphasis on quantitative, "hard" techniques to the exclusion of the "softer," interpersonal skills.[2]

These new management views are much closer to how most members of university faculties and administrations idealize management issues. While traditional management theory has stressed the analysis and manipulation of data to support *decisions,* Peters and Waterman define management activity more broadly. Their focus on *pathfinding* and *implementation* activities, "softer" and less rational techniques, more closely describes what it is that faculties expect their presidents, provosts, deans, and department chairpersons to do.

Those who have chosen to enter the world of academia are likely to agree with Philip Selznick's observation that "Organizations become institutions as they are infused with values."[3] Men and women join university faculties for a variety of reasons. The university, like all organizations, is a complex collection of paradox and ambiguity. Exclusive focus on individual goals, without commitment to shared values, weakens the sense of institution and community, contributes to a vague, but often persistent, sense of individual and collective anxiety, and denies the individual's need to identify with nontransient and lasting values. Exclusive focus on collective achievement ignores the individual's desire to be recognized, to stand apart from the masses, to think and act for himself or herself, and to realize his or her full potential. The excellent organization is one that creates a culture of shared basic values and an environment that encourages individual achievement and recognition.

III.

How successful have universities been in providing an environment that encourages individual and institutional development? During the halcyon days of the sixties many institutions of higher education seem to have lost a strong sense of collective purpose. Instead of identifying and articulating basic values, many university leaders focused their attention on attaining short-term, tangible measures of success. The culture became more growth- and numbers-oriented. Growth in numbers of students, budgets, and buildings became the measure of organizational success. Instead of focusing on the goals that the budgets and buildings would help to achieve, the leaders frequently confused means with ends.

Faculty numbers expanded and respect for individual differences diminished. All too often the critical contribution of the "rank-and-file" faculty member to the achievement of excellence in a university's teaching, research, and service programs was lost as new administrative structures were created to accommodate rapid growth. Unionization of faculties, institution of formula funding, and a belief that scholarship could be adequately measured by number of publications further reinforced the view that if something could not be reduced to quantitative measurement, it was not consistent with the goal of institutional excellence.

For many faculty members, a lessened sense of collective mission and individual worth within the university led to an increased identification with the collective goals of a growing number of increasingly narrow disciplines. With the professor's ability to change institutional affiliation enhanced in a "seller's" market, career progression became identified more and more with job changing and prestige within the discipline rather than within the organization. As early as 1958 the tendency for professors to think of themselves as disciplinary scholars, rather than as university or college educators, was identified and documented by Caplow and McGee in their thought-provoking book, *The Academic Marketplace.*[4]

During this period many of the nation's corporations were also caught up in the same mindless rush to get bigger. Conglomerate merger fever led corporations to acquire diverse and unrelated businesses. Bigger was better. The belief in economies of management scale was everywhere. Organizational mission was defined in terms of standardizing, accounting, capital budgeting, and financial control systems. Career progression was associated more with the individual's functional specialization—accounting, law, marketing, and so forth—than with his contribution to the corporate mission or to the creation of a quality product. Robert Hayes and William Abernathy, reflecting upon these developments, argue that recent American management theory and practice may have significantly contributed to our competitive decline in the world marketplace. They suggest that it is time for management to return to the basic task of producing value through providing high-quality products and services that meet and anticipate society's future needs.[5]

Many universities, too, in their attempts to grow and be all things to all people, undertook new and diverse activities that often were consistent only with the goal of getting bigger. There are striking similarities between the growth of large conglomerate corporations and the growth of the "multiversity" concept. There was a tendency to expand into new activities that were not well understood and were relatively far removed from the basic "business" of the university. Establishing policies and procedures consistent with a higher sense of mission—one based on clearly articulated and well-understood shared values—was given a low priority. Regional universities simultaneously attempted to build nationally recognized, comprehensive doctoral programs in all fields and to increase undergraduate enrollments by relaxing admission standards. The desire to build scholarly excellence by attracting sponsored research and a nationally recognized research faculty frequently stood in stark contrast with a willingness to accept low-quality undergraduate instruction. Class size grew, faculties were encouraged to teach less (on the assumption that teaching less meant researching more), and, all too often, undergraduate programs were used to generate revenue to support weak graduate and research activities.

In retrospect, the results in both the corporate and educational sectors were all too predictable. Quality suffered and the "rank and file" became less motivated to strive for and achieve excellence in their day-to-day activities. While top management frequently was richly rewarded for the achievement of rapid growth, the people responsible for the fundamental work of the organization became less able to identify with distant corporate goals. Commitment to organizational growth provided little inspiration and guidance for their contributions. Management attention was focused more on gimmicks and financial sleight of hand than on inspiring, motivating, and nurturing a culture with clear values that would create an institution and not just a bigger organization.

IV.

The future environment is not likely to be as hospitable to exclusively growth-oriented strategies for either corporations or universities. Managing for growth in numbers may have been a viable, if not wise, strategy for the sixties and the seventies. Continuation of a strategy of managing by the numbers rather than through shared values will prove to be fatal in the late eighties.

Slowing productivity growth, increased foreign competition, and the deregulation of many key industries are forcing firms to assess more carefully what they do and how they do it. The much-cited decline in the traditional college-age population and its changing racial and ethnic composition make a continued emphasis on growth strategy highly problematic for colleges and universities. For example, some states will experience as much as a 30 to 40 percent decline in the number of high school graduates who traditionally attend college.[6] While some institutions seem to have adopted strategies built upon the assumption that declining numbers of seventeen- to twenty-one-year-olds will affect every other institution but theirs, others have wisely begun to scale back their enrollment projections.

In addition to purely demographic factors, other changes are likely to occur that will further lessen the desirability and feasibility of pursuing a growth-oriented, "business-as-usual," strategy. For example:

- The "vocational" value of a college education has been declining and is likely to continue to do so for some time. The 1960s ability to "sell" a college education as a good investment will pay handsome private returns to the owners of a college diploma has been seriously weakened. Economic estimates of the private rates of return have been falling. Although Carolyn Bird's *The Case Against College* is overdrawn and misses the point that college education has an important social dimension, she is at least partially correct in arguing that if private gain is the only motivation for college attendance, fewer individuals should choose college.[7]

• The striking growth in the number of alternative sources of education and training is likely to further decrease the demand for traditional four-year undergraduate education. Community colleges and in-house corporate education programs for adults have made, and are likely to continue to make, relatively significant inroads. Those who are optimistic that growth in the demand for "lifelong learning" will offset the decline in demand from traditional-age students frequently tend to ignore the tremendous growth in the supply of nontraditional institutional suppliers.

• The public's new demands for increased educational rigor and excellence in grades K through 12 will lead to increased competition for government support of higher education. At the same time, new social demands for increased government support for activities unrelated to education, such as health care and social security (reflecting sharply shifting demographics on aging), will likely decrease the relative importance of educational issues on the national agenda in coming years.

• As undergraduate enrollments drop, graduate enrollments will also decline, since doctoral recipients in many fields are essentially prepared only for academic careers. Declining numbers of graduate enrollments are also likely to lead to a reduction in the number of truly outstanding research universities as limited government and corporate funds will be directed toward an increasingly small number of excellent programs enrolling a majority of the most promising graduate-degree candidates.

V.

Faced with future challenges such as these, what can universities learn from excellently managed corporations? One characteristic Peters and Waterman found to be dominant in the excellent companies was a bias toward action. Excellent companies are managed to encourage their people to work together to identify opportunities, to formulate plans, and most importantly, to act. People are encouraged to stay in touch with each other through informal and seemingly unstructured interaction. Managers rely less on formal reporting systems than on walking around, talking with the organization's members, and identifying and encouraging opportunities for action. Massive staff studies and highly structured reporting and sign-off systems are absent. The excellent company avoids the trap of paralysis through analysis. Peters and Waterman report one manager describing his organization's action bias by saying, "Do it, fix it, try it." Another expression of an action orientation was, "Ready, fire, aim."

Many observers of the academic world would no doubt conclude that faculty and university administrators are far from action-oriented. Stories abound of how faculty governing bodies study, debate, and more often than not opt for no action. Frequently, lack of faculty action reflects an unexamined commitment to what might be called the "status quo plus." During times of rapid growth, the status quo could be maintained, plus many new activities could be added to existing programs without serious disruption and/or debate. Faculty action, while desirable, was not critical. However, in the years ahead, both faculty and administrative action will require trading off among program goals rather than conveniently trading up to larger scale.

Are faculties inherently biased against action? In years past it probably was true that individuals who chose academic careers were looking for the "quiet," contemplative life. However, faculty members hired in the 1970s are as a group far more inclined to be judged by their actions and to take risks. As tenure standards tightened in the past decade or so and the prospects for institutional growth dimmed, the decision to pursue a career in academia was, and still is, increasingly a decision to take risks and accept the challenge of being an active (publishing?) scholar and teacher. Although the philosophical dichotomy between thought and action is still recognized by many, the influence of pragmatic, action-oriented philosophies, has increased.

The description of how excellently managed firms structure their activity, the informality of communication, and the managers' commitment to gathering information are strikingly similar to that found in many excellent academic departments. These departments are able to meet new course demands, to respond to requests for research proposals, and formulate a variety of actions in a timely manner. "Do it, fix it, try it" frequently describes how departmentally controlled affairs are approached. Unfortunately, things are not so structured at the school, college, or university level.

There seem to be several managerial impediments to action beyond the department level. First of all, in the absence of a well-articulated and widely held statement of institutional mission, faculties are given little specific guidance or incentive to act. As a consequence, the disciplinary values of departmental faculty tend to direct departmental action. Any action requiring cooperation and coordination across disciplines is likely to suffer. Thus, for example, teaching courses for nonmajors, advisement of nonmajors, general education curricula, and a host of other issues that need attention tend to suffer from benign neglect.

In the coming decade, academic deans, vice-presidents, and presidents must devise mechanisms whereby individual faculty actions that benefit the entire institution are more strongly encouraged. Upper-level administrators should become more familiar with the day-to-day activities of the faculty by walking around, teaching classes, and encouraging interdepartmental interaction.

The internal allocation of resources and individual rewards needs to be more explicitly related to actions that foster the attainment of institutional goals. The simple use of funding formulas for department budgets tied to the number of majors, credit hours, and the like begs the central question as to what the institution is fundamentally about. While the direct output of a department should be measured clearly and taken into account when allocating resources, so should the department's indirect contribution to the overall goals of a university. Creative, mission-oriented, rather than departmentally based, information systems, are likely to emerge that more clearly identify the allocation of resources to collective, interdepartmental activities such as general education. It is highly unlikely, however, that precise quantitative adminstrative guidelines can be, or should be, developed. The success of any effort to encourage a broader institutional action focus will be directly related to administrators' willingness and ability to exercise academic and managerial judgment within the constraints of the shared value system.

During the growth period, counterproductive, complicated, and extensive reporting and control systems were frequently imposed upon universities from external sources. A variety of government-inspired regulations dealing with accounting for sponsored research activities, affirmative action, and other social-purpose legislation, as well as higher demands for accountability by trustees and state legislatures, immediately come to mind. The response to these demands has given rise to an administrative bureaucracy that all too often creates significant barriers to faculty action. Worse yet, the creative action-oriented talents of faculty are misdirected toward creative but mainly nonproductive actions to "beat the system."

Undesirable, externally imposed control often followed from the upper-level administration's desire to grow and its willingness to undertake diverse new programs that had heavy, hidden administrative costs. In the absence of a well-defined and understood sense of mission and shared values, it is readily understandable why external agencies demand bureaucratic measures of accountability. It is also the case that in the absence of a clear sense of university purpose, accountability tends to focus on the deployment of inputs rather than the achievement of mutually desired results—results that are likely to be poorly understood and not embraced by the university itself.

Before new programs and sources of funding are sought or accepted, university administrators would be wise to require a bureaucratic "environmental impact" statement. Too many times Trojan horses, often requiring the allocation of matching funds, are foolishly acquired. Too often projects that are rationalized on the basis of contributing to the growth of teaching, research, or service contribute more to overhead and the creation of a nonaction-oriented environment rather than to fostering basic academic values.

The tendency for faculty and administrators to create committees and task-force assignments that are charged with studying problems rather than with finding and implementing solutions also contributes to a lack of action orientation. Following Peters and Waterman's observations, if and when action is desired, committee members should be chosen so that they will have a reasonable opportunity to implement (and live with) any committee recommendations that are accepted. Committee members should have a good understanding of what is expected and when it is expected. Members should be interested in the task and be willing volunteers. If committee and task-force assignments lead to little more than scoring debating points and do not have any impact on action, action-oriented people will avoid serving. Instead, a new class of bureaucrat, the perennial faculty committee member, will serve with indistinction.

Another characteristic of excellent corporations is that they tend to stay close to their customers. As Peters and Waterman observe, "These companies learn from the people they serve."[8] So should it be with higher education. Faculty and adminstrators too often measure the value of their contributions through measuring the value of the inputs into the educational process rather than the *value added* by the process. Too often educational success is measured by the SAT scores of entering freshmen and not by assessing the personal and intellectual growth that occurs over four years. Scholarly contributions are measured by dollars of sponsored research and by publication rates rather than by a careful assessment of the significance of the contribution to society's fund of knowledge and its relationship to the educational and service missions of the university.

Staying close to the customer means ascertaining the accomplishments of alumni, seeking out students' evaluations of their educational experience, and soliciting the assessment of research and graduate efforts by industry and other users of the university's end products. Surveys conducted by centralized administrative staff offices can gather a good deal of information and can be of real value in encouraging all members of the university to learn more from and about the people they serve. However, faculty and administrator contact with alumni, current and future students and their parents, representatives of government and industry, and foundation groups, may be even more effective. Meetings with boards of visitors or advisory councils can help to clarify what a program has accomplished, what end-users might want to accomplish, and how the program meets, or does not meet, the needs of the people it serves. Such self-evaluation can also help the members of the organization to identify and articulate their shared values and to ascertain how well they have been served.

Seeing ourselves as others see us can be most instructive. But successful organizations, especially during periods of rapid change, such as that facing higher education, must do much more than simply ask what customers want today and then provide it. Excellent organizations encourage all their people to identify and champion new programs and activities that meet future needs only dimly seen in the present. Entrepreneurial activity, the ability to identify worthwhile new activities before others do, is the key to maintaining a dynamic organization. Whether it is the professor discovering and implementing better and more cost-effective ways to teach music using computer-aided instruction, or the corporate engineer developing a new automated clinical analyzer, the process is remarkably similar. They both need to be encouraged to think about what their customers really need and how the need might be better met, and to strike out on their own and do it. The creative and inquiring minds of a faculty firmly grounded in an understanding of the institution's values and mission, coupled with a better understanding of society's expectations and an action-orientated environment, can provide innovative responses to ever-changing circumstances.

VI.

Few academics would challenge the view that the source of any university's excellence is, at base, to be found in the talents and accomplishments of its faculty. Peters and Waterman's discovery of the critical importance of the individual contributions of the members of the corporation reaffirms what has been professed, if not always believed, for decades in academia. The faculty is, in some real sense, the university. Unfortunatley, as the desire to measure success through growth became more prominent in higher education, many institutions lost sight of the simple truth that an organization is not likely to be much better than the people who do its day-to-day work.

As higher education enters a more competitive environment in the years ahead, greater recognition must be given to the reality that professionals, faculty, staff, and administrators are all faced with a common challenge—to assure that their unique institution and its values survive and thrive in a new and different world. Confrontation and distrust need to be lessened and greater co-operation and participation engendered. The actions of all groups within the university, especially administrators, must be judged by how they foster (or retard) the attainment of the collective goals of the institution. While individual autonomy can and must be fostered, the excellent university and the excellent corporation must both be "fanatic centralists around the few core values they hold dear."

The guiding principles for excellently managed corporations are remarkably similar to those likely to be found in the world of academia. Respect for the power of ideas and the worth of the individual, a recognition that complex control and reporting mechanisms stifle creativity, a commitment to discovery, a realization that success cannot be measured by short-term results alone, a belief that institutions and individuals can both react to and act upon their environment, and a recognition of the importance of collective activity—all these are ideas that can be held by the academy and the excellently managed corporation. While there may not be a "bottom line" in the not-for-profit university, the path to achieving success may be more similar to than different from that found in the corporate world.

NOTES

1. Thomas J. Peters and Robert H. Waterman, Jr., *In Search of Excellence: Lessons from America's Best-Run Companies* (New York: Harper and Row, 1982).

2. Anthony G. Athos and Richard Tanner Pascale, *The Art of Japanese Management* (New York: Warner Books, 1981).

3. Cited in Peters and Waterman, *In Search of Excellence*, pp. 98-99.

4. Theodore Caplow and Reece J. McGee, *The Academic Marketplace* (Garden City, New York: Anchor Books, Inc., 1965).

5. Robert Hayes and William Abernathy, "Managing Our Way to Economic Decline," *Harvard Business Review* (July-August 1980).

6. Fred E. Crossland, "Learning to Cope with a Downward Slope," *Change* (July/August 1980), pp. 18-25.

7. Carolyn Bird, *The Case Against College* (New York: D. McKay Co., 1975).

8. Peters and Waterman, *In Search of Excellence*, p. 14.

9. Ibid., p. 15.

C. Harold Brown and Linda Tom

People and Productivity in the American University

Introduction

Universities and colleges, like business corporations, are highly complex organizations and, as such, require a strong and well-defined management function to accomplish their institutional goals. Higher education has experienced many significant changes in the last three decades—all of which have tended to increase structural and operational complexity and raise new management issues and problems. The early postwar years were a period of dramatic growth, which saw enrollment at private institutions more than double—from 1.1 million students to 2.5 million—by 1980. Within the same thirty-year span, enrollments at public institutions rocketed from 1.1 to 9 million students.[1] The tremendous growth in enrollments was reflected in a major expansion of existing colleges and universities as well as in the establishment of new institutions. Not surprisingly, this boom led to increasingly complex organizational structures as ever-larger institutions gathered a wider and wider range of schools, departments, programs, activities, and support services under a single administrative umbrella. In addition, external (e.g., social and government) forces presented colleges and universities with a far more diverse student population and a broad range of sensitive new issues—from civil rights to occupational health and safety—which required management expertise in wholly new areas and at a level not previously demanded in traditional ones.

The unprecedented surge in demand for postsecondary education in the years following the Second World War was not, however, destined to continue. Indeed, since the late 1970s campuses across the country have begun to experience declining enrollments and growing financial problems, with no expectation for a reversal of this trend in the near future. In view of current economic realities, "University managers have recognized that they must be as concerned with the bottom line as business firms. The latter want to make their profits as large as possible, while the university wants to be in the black."[2] Moreover, this new period of retrenchment is occurring at a time when the academic profession appears to be losing ground relative to other occupations in terms of prestige and compensation. All this has prompted one commentator to describe the American university in the 1980s as "an increasingly endangered species."[3] And as colleges and universities face less money but greater pressures to maintain high-quality teaching and research programs, we can anticipate that the situation will become even more difficult. Changing demographic and economic patterns point to the urgent need for developing sound management policies and practices—geared to the specific aims and organizational character of higher education—which will allow American universities and colleges to maintain excellence in the decades ahead.

While effective management is as indispensable to the academic as to the business world, the unique purpose (the advancement and transmission of knowledge) and traditions of higher education strongly influence its organizational structure in distinctive ways that should not be overlooked. The particular traditions and institutional nature of the academy are based on the essential "freedom of the masters to determine who would teach and what would be taught."[4] As affirmed by the United States Supreme Court, "the four essential freedoms of a university are to determine for itself on academic grounds who may teach, what may be taught, how it shall be taught and who may be admitted to study."[5] Much of the knowledge and authority relative to teaching and research reside with faculty, department chairpersons, and deans. Accordingly, various personnel decisions, such as promotion and tenure, often flow from them. This unique culture of higher education dictates an organizational structure that is decentralized and heterogeneous.

The decentralized structure characteristic of and necessary to academic institutions in no way diminishes the value of the management component. On the contrary, effective management is even more complex and critical in decentralized and hetergeneous organizations. Nevetheless, there appears to be an inherent philosophical rejection of the application of management science techniques to universities. It is an interesting paradox that "despite the fact that management science was born in academia, university managers have been slow to apply the techniques to the problems of their institutions."[6] This paradox may be explained when we consider that universities and colleges are typified by a "value system that rejects the technocratic, reveres the creative, and thereby delegitimatizes the practice of management . . . ."[7] Yet it is essential to develop a new value orientation that is compatible with the mission and traditions of higher education but at the same time encourages the use of sound management practices as a normal part of running the university. The management component will have to be accorded much greater importance in the value system, and necessary resources will have to be allocated for ongoing management development if universities are to uphold their mission and traditions in the face of the problems and realities of the coming decades.

Further, if academic adminstrators are to succeed in meeting the challenges that confront them, they will have to combine a commitment to the academic mission with the ability and willingness to learn and implement innovative approaches to administration. The following three programmatic recommendations will be examined: 1) establishment of a strong human resource development capability with a progressive and flexible orientation; 2) creation of an environment that will motivate faculty and staff to attain their highest levels of creativity and productivity; and 3) development and implementation of an effective ongoing training and development program for academic administrators.

Creation of a Strong Human Resource Capability

The importance of the individual worker in the overall scheme of business profitability has become a central corporate issue. Increased attention to human resource development and the growing numbers of corporate planning and development positions involving every phase of human resources attest to the high degree of concern by upper-level management. Universities are by their nature labor intensive and must rely heavily on human resources. Yet, unlike business and industry, there are few universities that have recognized the management of human resources at an institutional level within the central administration. While there are vice-presidents for academic affairs and student affairs, there are few vice-presidents for human resources. A commentator on the subject of academic adminstration recently made the following astute observation:

> Almost no major business is without a vice-president for human resource development. While colleges have not reflected the importance of human resources in their organizational chart, human resources have always been the principal wealth of colleges and universities, even when financial and physical resources were far more plentiful. As with other resources, human resources need conservation and nurturing.[8]

The University of Delaware is probably unique in having established a vice-president for human resource administration. The position is also unusual in that the incumbent is an academician—a former faculty member and dean.

The importance of the human resource component is probably a more salient feature in a university setting than in other organizations because the main "business" of higher education—academic programs—is fundamentally a people-centered activity. Academic programs are carried out by faculty in classrooms and laboratories. These functions are reinforced by professional staff who work in research capacities as well as in administrative areas. Faculty and professionals are complemented by support staff who provide indispensable clerical, technical, and physical plant functions. Most work is performed in a setting that involves a great deal of social interaction, and effective interpersonal skills are thus essential in getting the job done. Since the university's personnel resources are so clearly vital to its mission, the ability to acquire and maintain a quality faculty and professional and support staff directly impacts the quality of academic programs and success in meeting teaching, research, and service objectives. It is not surprising that the largest part of a university's budget is invested in personnel and employment-related costs.

The primary goals of the human resource function should be to provide services and programs that: 1) attract high quality people—faculty, professionals, and support staff; 2) enhance the ability of individuals to perform their work by providing adequate training and appropriate support; and 3) develop and maintain a responsive and positive environment conducive to the highest levels of productivity. In accomplishing these goals, individuals need to feel adequately compensated, fairly treated, and meaningfully involved in decisions and issues that affect them and their work. Essential to the success of these objectives is an underlying management philosophy that assumes people will be most productive if they are trusted, supported, and valued.

This philosophy has gained broad appeal as reported in research conducted by Thomas Peters and Robert Waterman in their "search of excellence"—a theme frequently heard in the halls of academe. Peters and Waterman studied the management practices of successful corporations throughout the country and reported some of the principal "lessons from America's best-run companies":

> Treat people as adults. Treat them as partners; treat them with
> dignity; treat them with respect . . . . These are the fundamental
> lessons from the excellent companies . . . . In other words, if you
> want productivity . . . you must treat your workers as your most
> important asset . . . . There was hardly a more pervasive theme in
> the excellent companies than respect for the individual. That basic
> belief and assumption were omnipresent.[9]

The theme of respect appears to have a natural affinity to
institutions of higher education, whose emphasis is on contributions of individuals as scholars and teachers. A recent Carnegie
Foundation report on higher education concluded:

> Like all human institutions, the academy can be no greater than
> the human beings who comprise it. For all the attention to flow
> charts, master plans, and program reviews, the educational enter-
> prise ultimately depends upon people.[10]

The "people" principles espoused by Peters and Waterman need
to be pursued with as much vigor in the university as in the
business sector. The management philosophy crucial to human
resource development stresses trust and respect for the individual.
Effective managers are those men and women who try to help
individuals feel good about themselves and about the work they do
at the institution. Every effort must be made to provide opportunities for the individual to demonstrate his or her capabilities. This
approach is not indulging in mushy thinking. Persons who are
satisfied in their work are more productive employees. In this
context, then, managers really make two major kinds of management decisions. The first and perhaps most significant decision is
whom to hire. The objective clearly is to find and retain the most
qualified and competent individuals. Once hired, employees should
be assumed to be trustworthy and motivated and to possess initiative. Since hiring mistakes occur occasionally, the second most
important managerial decision is whom to keep. If employees
demonstrate that they are not capable, not trustworthy, that they
have neither the mind, the hand, nor the eye for the task, then they

should be helped to leave the university. This can be done within an atmosphere of respect and civility.

In sum, the specific form and substance of a human resource development program will depend on the socio-cultural heritage unique to each particular institution. The two primary prerequisites, however, for any effective human resource management program are: first, that the institution formulate and adopt a clearly articulated human resource management philosophy that emphasizes the value and contributions of individual employees; and second, that a competent and well-administered human resource capability or function be established to develop and implement innovative programs suited to the organization. For these things to happen, the issues of human resource development must be placed high enough on the institutional agenda so that they receive attention at the uppermost levels within the university.

Development of a Positive and Responsive Work Environment

Effective management involves creation of a work environment that motivates people to attain their highest levels of creativity and productivity. To foster a positive work climate, it is essential to establish a shared set of institutional values. From these values a mission statement specifying agreed-upon goals can be developed. Further, people want to participate in decisions that affect them in the workplace. They want to know what is going on and why. Everyone needs to feel that his or her job provides a chance for change, for advancement, or for personal and professional development. An environment that will motivate people to do their best is one in which everyone shares a set of common values, communicates openly and freely with each other, participates in activities in the workplace, and feels a part of an innovative and creative enterprise. It is undoubtedly difficult to create this environment ". . . when the faculty is demoralized, when administrators feel over-burdened and under-appreciated, and when avoiding crises is the role of educational leaders."[11]

Much has been written and said about goal setting in complex bureaucracies. In the goal-setting process, there must be agreement first as to what the values are that undergird the effort and serve as the glue for the social system. In a university setting a number of value streams flow within the institution. Some degree of consensus is necessary as to what the key values are, and these must be clearly communicated to everyone. In other words, to get where one wants to go there must be agreement on the destination. There can be arguments as to preferred routes or modes of transportation, but the direction and destination must be clear. Development of mission statements for universities, colleges, and departments, while desirable, is, unfortunately, much like the weather: it is often discussed, but little is done about it.

In effectively managed organizations, there is an ease in communications, both informally and formally. Simply put, people talk to each other about the things that matter. It is ironic that in universities, organizations in which communication skills are an important criterion for employment, actual communication is frequently lacking. For example, peer reviews, performance appraisals, program evaluations, and similar activities often are not openly communicated to affected personnel. More often than not administrators fail to discuss with their employees the tasks associated with their jobs or to indicate how well an individual is doing and how he or she might improve job performance. In academia, much attention is given to rewarding meritorious performance. Yet, little effort is made to communicate to the employee the relationship between performance and personnel actions such as salary increases and promotability. The administrator often finds this activity uncomfortable and bothersome; therefore, it is not done well, if at all. In many instances, small problems become matters of high principle because appropriate conversations do not take place early on to clarify the situation and to solve the problems. This is particularly true when the administrator has to "send a bad message." Talking with employees not only increases the likelihood of resolving problems at the earliest possible point—before they develop into serious conflicts—but is an effective way of keeping people well informed and encouraging them to "buy-in" to the goals of the system.

A prevailing value today is that people want to participate in decisions that affect them in the workplace. The governing structures of most institutions of higher learning reflect the faculty's desire for an active part in making decisions affecting academic issues. Faculty senates and college and department committees, for example, are forums that afford faculty members an opportunity to participate in a wide spectrum of academic matters. The value of participation and involvement is emphasized in a Carnegie Foundation report on governance of higher education:

> The best measure of the health of the governance structure is not how it looks on paper, but the climate in which it functions. Do those involved see some point to what they are doing? Do they believe their efforts can make a difference? Is there a sense of excitement?[12]

And in a recent study of fourteen private colleges that were experiencing significant financial difficulties, schools that recovered fairly quickly and fully were described as follows:

> In establishing limits and goals, in setting forth criteria for judging progress, in defining organizational identity, the administration neither dictates to the faculty nor gives the faculty carte blanche. The decision process is marked by a high degree of communication and openness between the administration and the faculty. Faculty commitment to the administration's statement of institutional goals and operational policies arises from this involvement in organizational processes.[13]

The desire to participate has become so strong that, in recent years, unions have been formed among faculty at some institutions. Unionization often occurs when administrators are autocratic and the faculty believe that they can be better represented through collective bargaining.[14] In these situations, the environment is typically characterized by lack of effective communication, and fac-

ulty members are not meaningfully involved or allowed to participate in affairs of consequence to the institution. Adversary and
conflicting relationships are likely to evolve between the administration and the faculty. The existence of collective bargaining does
not reduce the need for effective communication and participation.
In fact, the need is even more critical because unionization is
commonly a sign that channels of communication are impaired.
The presence of a union ought not be used as an excuse to avoid
the responsibilities of effective management.

In so far as contract negotiations are usually the most dramatic
part of the collective bargaining process, they receive the most
public attention. It is important to emphasize, however, that the
quality of the relationship between management and employees
depends upon how a contract is administered, not how it is nego-
tiated. That is, how well do the parties get along during the life of
the contract? In fact, the quality of the labor-management relationship generally dictates the nature of negotiations. The collective bargaining relationship between unions and the administration is mature when it is characterized by high levels of trust and
civility. This can occur when the union leadership and the central
administration communicate openly and regularly on matters of
common interest in order to resolve problems as they arise. In
most instances, problems can be resolved in a cooperative and
informal fashion when there is ongoing dialogue between the leadership of the union and the administration. This is not to suggest
that all differences will result in consensus. On occasion the parties will disagree on matters of principle. The important lesson
here is that reasonable people can disagree and still maintain respect for one another.

The situation is more complicated, however, when a faculty
union and a faculty senate are present on the same campus. Then
there is potential for conflict and confusion of roles. Yet these
problems can be minimized if certain distinctions are kept in mind.
The modes of decision making associated with faculty unions and
faculty senates are quite different. While collective bargaining is
often adversarial, a faculty senate's decisions are typically arrived

at through open exchange of viewpoints and debate carried out in a collegial environment. Differences between faculty and academic administrators are in fact so much blurred in the collegial model associated with faculty senate proceedings that the Supreme Court ruled in the Yeshiva case that faculty at private institutions resemble management and therefore are precluded from bargaining rights under the National Labor Relations Act. Now, as the modes of decision making differ, so, too, should the issues they deal with. The matter of jurisdiction as to which issues are appropriate to the senate and which to the bargaining table can be fraught with difficult conflicts unless the parties concerned define and accept jurisdictions appropriate to each group. Traditionally, the faculty senate has dealt with matters involving academic judgment and the union has represented faculty on economic matters and conditions of employment. This separation offers a viable compromise between collective bargaining and the traditional governing structure found in universities. It could be argued that the presence of a strong and effective faculty senate and the use of the collegial model would preclude the need for collective bargaining. Nevertheless, since faculty unions have been created alongside senate structures (often for reasons idiosyncratic to the particular institutions), they should be considered a fact of life where they exist.

In our judgment, unions are not the most effective way to deal with problems and issues that confront the academic community. This is probably most pertinent with respect to faculty. While faculty compensation and rewards have undergone a steady erosion over the last decade, collective bargaining has not become the prevalent approach to deal with these problems. Studies of collective bargaining in higher education that have examined both public and private schools indicate the existence of a broad consensus among faculty and administrators in favor of harmonious relationships based on mutual respect and collegiality. More often than not, the faculty and the adminsitration share a dedication to the mission and goals of the institution. Collective bargaining is not generally regarded as a desirable or an effective organizational strategy.[15]

If real opportunities are created for people to participate in decisons that affect them in the workplace and an ease of communication exists among the administration, the faculty, and the staff, then many of the problems that lead to the formation of unions will be minimized. Of course some university professionals and support staff neither participate in faculty senates and college and department committees nor are represented by unions. Yet these groups, too, must be given opportunities for participation. Elected, representative advisory councils are one of the ways to achieve greater involvement of nonfaculty personnel. These councils enable employee groups to identify problems, propose solutions, and communicate their concerns directly to the central administration. At the same time, the councils provide effective mechanisms for information-sharing back to the employee groups from the central administration. Creation of task forces, committees, or other ad hoc groups to deal with issues of institutional concern are additional ways of providing opportunities for participation. Multiple efforts, both formal and informal, are needed to provide as many opportunities as possible for people to be actively involved in the affairs of the institution.

Given the probable decline in enrollments and the limited commitment of financial and other resources, it is assumed that most universities will remain in a relatively stable state. This suggests that innovative ways must be sought during the current period of cutback to make university jobs sufficiently attractive so that people are motivated to be creative and productive. Kanter argues persuasively that university managers must create work environments in which people perceive their jobs as providing opportunities for accomplishment and which empower them to get the job done.[16] Development of clarified career paths in which the steps for promotion are clear and attainable is one way to generate a motivational work climate. Defined career paths help individuals anticipate and prepare for successive steps that involve growth and challenge.[17] Other ideas such as job sharing and job rotation need to be explored. Lateral transfers may be utilized to provide fresh challenges in new fields when promotion is not possible.

More frequent and explicit use of temporary assignments and outside service activities can also provide opportunities for challenge and change, even if on a temporary basis. These types of opportunities are beginning to be made available to faculty, but should be expanded to include administrators and other professionals.

Training and Development for Academic Managers

Certain paradoxes concerning effective management of human resources have become evident. One obvious paradox is that while universities exist for the provision of learning and human development, they often do not provide adequate learning and growth opportunities for their own employees. As one observer has commented, "lifelong learning is far more available to students and to the community than it is to those who provide it."[18] Another paradox is that the faculty route into administration is the most common path, but the criteria for making one eligible for an administrative job are not the same as the skills needed to do the job. Generally, members of university communities are selected to be administrators on the basis of their academic credentials. There is little formal preparation for the new role. The expectation is that the scholar will learn the administrative job by actually doing it. Experience has shown, however, that accomplished scholars do not always make effective administrators. Careful reassessment of traditional assumptions concerning selection criteria and training of academic managers is imperative. There can be little doubt that "In the coming years, educators will have to abandon the notion—or rather relinquish the wish—that the art of administration requires little if any training."[19]

In many instances faculties view "administration" simply as a necessary evil. They often act as if they undertake administrative duties as fulfillment of their service obligations and look forward to returning to the classroom and laboratory as soon as possible. Because of their negative attitudes toward administration, academicians are slow to acknowledge the need for professional development and training in this area. Higher education spends little money or effort in the development of its academic managers. By comparison, resources dedicated to the training effort in business and industry are significant. A Conference Board publication in 1977 noted that a total of $1.6 billion was allocated for training programs in industry; of this total, a major portion was for executive development.[20] In universities in which employee-training functions do exist, most training is for clerical staff and other nonacademic employees.

There is some evidence that a recognition of the need for training and development of academic administrators is beginning to take hold. More programs are being offered through the American Council on Education and similar professional organizations. Presidents, vice-presidents, deans, and chairpersons are those who benefit from these programs. However, it is also necessary to develop ongoing in-house training and development programs for all levels and groups of university administrators. In-house programs should articulate the unique characteristics of the institution and respond to its particular needs. In these efforts, resources within the university should be fully exploited. There is, for example, an enormous wealth of expertise in business schools and other academic departments that can be utilized.

Training programs need to be developed and provided in all major areas of administration, including: 1) leadership and motivation, 2) interpersonal skills development, 3) program development/planning, 4) financial and budget administration, 5) decision making, 6) performance appraisal, 7) employment practices, and 8) legal issues. Each is discussed briefly below.

Leadership and Motivational Skills: The ability of the administrator to produce and sustain high levels of commitment to and confidence in the institution among employees is essential, particularly in difficult and uncertain times when institutional resources are limited and anxiety levels are heightened. A recent study concluded that "a private college may survive poor leadership, but it cannot rise above it."[21] Training in this area should include discussion of leadership styles and motivational theory.

Interpersonal Skills Development: The administrator in the 1980s will have to be effective in handling conflict situations at a time when the support and confidence of the many constituencies of the university must be vigorously pursued. This involves interaction not only with faculty, staff, students, and parents; but also with legislators, prospective students, government bureaucrats, citizens, donors, and alumni. Training in this area should focus on communication, negotiation skills, approaches to conflict resolution, analysis of interpersonal conflict, and development of problem-solving skills.

Program Development/Planning: With leaner budgets, decisions relative to changes or reductions in programs require sound judgments, the capacity and willingness to innovate, accurate assessment of needs and effects, and appropriate follow-through measures. Training activities in this area should include goal setting, needs assessment, integration of academic and fiscal planning, and modes of employee participation.

Financial and Budget Administration: Training in this area should provide greater understanding of the fundamentals of the budgetary process and of the need to formulate budget decisions in accordance with planned objectives. In-house training programs should focus on the financial and budgetary systems of the institution.

Decision making: Administrators are involved in situations on a day-to-day basis in which they are required to make decisions affecting a variety of issues. Training in this area should focus on enhancement of decision-making capabilities through examination and understanding of different styles and approaches to effective decision making.

Performance Appraisal: Formal evaluation of employees, when used for making decisions pertaining to career growth, promotion and tenure, and salary is a critical part of the academic administrator's job, since these decisions significantly affect individuals' careers, morale, and general level of job fulfillment. The fact that decisions related to evaluations are being challenged more and more often through grievance procedures and legal channels underscores the need for training in this area. Training should focus on developing an understanding of the purpose of evaluation, sources of evaluative information, relevant institutional procedures and policies, and various ways to do evaluations.

Employment Practices: With values and expectations in the workforce changing to reflect employee demands for participation, open communication, career advancement, and the like, administrators must be able to deal openly with faculty and staff on all aspects of decisions affecting them. Management decisions relating to salaries, promotion, performance evaluation, and nonrenewal will be challenged more often. Administrators must be able to deal with performance-related problems promptly and openly, articulate defensible positions for their assessments and decisions, develop appropriate documentation to support their positions, and take timely and appropriate actions to ensure that problems are resolved. Training in this area should inform administrators of relevant university personnel policies and procedures as well as provide guidance on how to handle the sorts of employee problems most likely to occur.

Legal Issues: Academia is finding itself, as are other employers, involved more often in costly litigation as a result of growing numbers of statutory regulations and an increasingly litigious society. Administrators need to know the legal requirements pertaining to their administrative responsibilities and actions and to understand the potential legal ramifications of their decisions. Training should provide information on the various employment discrimination laws and other legislation relevant to employment, promotion, termination, performance evaluation, retirement, and similar matters. Focus should be placed on problem prevention and sound management practices.

In addition to traditional management training programs, efforts should be made to enhance communication among academic administrators within the university. These activities are valuable not only in the exchange of information and ideas, but also as a positive force for team-building.

Conclusion

A major challenge for the American university is to maintain its academic integrity in an environment of declining enrollments, inadequate budgets, increased external regulation, and, at best, a skeptical public. Achievement of institutional goals in the face of these pressures will require those within the academy to work together in a spirit of cooperation and with a shared sense of purpose. It appears that everyone will have to learn to "manage down." More will have to be accomplished with less. Growth can no longer be taken for granted. Collective decisions will have to be made to determine which programs to keep and which to eliminate. To make these decisions wisely and to implement them in a positive and constructive manner will require an institution-wide effort. The participation of everyone involved and affected within the campus community will be critical. As articulated in the Carnegie Foundation report on governance, "If campuses are not actively involved when tough decisions must be made, authority is drained, priorities become confused, morale plummets, and efficiency declines."[22] The challenges confronting us can be met only in an environment of high trust, respect, cooperation, and mutual assistance. Efforts to create such an environment will have to be an essential part of any long-term strategy of American universities as they seek to prosper in the difficult years ahead.

NOTES

1. Carnegie Foundation For the Advancement of Teaching, *The Control of the Campus, A Report on the Governance of Higher Education* (Washington, D.C., 1982), p. 37.

2. Richard M. Cyert, "Management Science and University Management," in *Management Science Applications to Academic Administration*, ed. James A. Wilson (San Francisco: Jossey-Bass Inc., 1981), p. 28.

3. Ibid., p. 40.

4. Carnegie Foundation, *Control of the Campus*, p. 5.

5. Ibid., p. 4.

6. Cyert, "Management Science and University Management," p. 27.

7. Madeleine F. Green, "Developing Leadership: A Paradox in Academe," in *Academic Leaders As Managers*, ed. Robert H. Atwell and Madeleine F. Green, (San Francisco: Jossey-Bass, Inc., 1981), p. 12.

8. Ibid., p. 16.

9. Thomas J. Peters and Robert H. Waterman, Jr., *In Search of Excellence: Lessons from America's Best-Run Companies* (New York: Harper and Row, 1982), p. 238.

10. Carnegie Foundation, *Control of the Campus*, p. 88.

11. Rosabeth Moss Kanter, "Changing the Shape of Work: Reform in Academe," (Plenary address to the American Association for Higher Education, Washington, D.C., 17 April 1979), p. 1.

12. Carnegie Foundation, *Control of the Campus*, p. 88.

13. Ellen Earle Chaffee, "The Human Element is the Bottom Line: The Confidence Factor and Institutional Vitality," (Paper delivered at 12th Annual Conference of the National Center for the Study of Collective Bargaining in Higher Education and the Professions, New York, 30 April 1984), p. 12.

14. Kenneth P. Mortimer and Richard C. Richardson, Jr., *Governance in Institutions With Faculty Unions: Six Case Studies* (University Park, Penn.: Center for the Study of Higher Education, Pennsylvania State University, 1977).

15. Chaffee, "The Human Element is the Bottom Line," p. 8.

16. Rosabeth Moss Kanter, *Men and Women of the Corporation*, (New York: Basic Books, 1977).

17. Robert A. Scott, *Lords, Squires, and Yeomen: Collegiate Middle Managers and Their Organizations*, (Washington, D.C.: American Association for Higher Education, 1978).

18. Green, "Developing Leadership," p. 12.

19. Ibid., p. 17.

20. S. Lusterman, *Education in Industry* (New York: The Conference Board, 1977).

21. Chaffee, "The Human Element is the Bottom Line," p. 9.

22. Carnegie Foundation, *Control of the Campus,* p. 43.

John A. Munroe

Afterword: A Short History of the University of Delaware

The University of Delaware traces its origin to a free school started by the Reverend Francis Alison at New London, Pennsylvania, in the fall of 1743. Alison was a Presbyterian minister, a graduate of the University of Edinburgh, who had come to America from his native Ireland in 1735 and was disturbed by the lack of preparatory and college-level schools to train young men for the professions, including the ministry.

Most Presbyterians in the Middle Atlantic colonies in 1743 were either immigrants or the children of immigrants from Ulster, the northern province of Ireland, where a large proportion of the population was of Scottish descent. Most of their American ministers were also immigrants, but as the Scotch-Irish population increased and spread westward from the coast, a problem arose in supplying sufficient numbers of ministers, particularly those with the educational background Presbyterians expected. In the emergency some zealous young men were being admitted to the ministry with little formal training, and the Lewes presbytery (made up of delegates from Presbyterian churches in the lower part of the Delmarva Peninsula) urged careful examination of the educational attainments of all candidates. This view represented the attitude of those who were called the "old side" Presbyterians; the "new side" put more emphasis on enthusiasm than on education, and the difference of opinion caused difficulties, even a temporary division among the American Presbyterians.

Francis Alison, a staunch member of the "old side" faction, began his own school at home, where he had already been tutoring a few students. In a very short time the governing Presbyterian body, the Synod of Philadelphia, adopted his school and encouraged the collection of funds in Presbyterian churches to support it. With this aid the school flourished, and its students, largely drawn from the vicinity, some living at home and some with the Alison family, eventually brought it renown.

When Alison left New London in January 1752 for a post in Philadelphia, his school was taken over by Alexander McDowell, another immigrant Presbyterian minister. McDowell moved the school to his home near Lewisville, Pennsylvania, but after about ten years it was moved to Newark, in the colony that became the State of Delaware. After the academy had been relocated in Newark, the "old side" Presbyterians conceived of developing it into a college as a rival to the "new side" College of New Jersey (later Princeton). Incorporation, with the power to grant degrees, depended on the Penn family, proprietors of Pennsylvania and Delaware; and Thomas Penn, the principal proprietor, having already approved a charter for a College of Philadelphia, refused to charter a second college.

The "old side" Presbyterians had to be content with the charter granted in 1769 for an Academy of Newark, but they soon resolved to make it a college in all but name. Both preparatory and college-level courses were taught, although only diplomas, not degrees, were granted. A two-story stone building had already been erected. Through their church connections, they recruited students from a wide area and sought funds from well-to-do Presbyterians in a still wider area, including distant colonies such as South Carolina and Jamaica as well as from England, Scotland, and Ireland. Two agents in England secured a gift for the Academy of Newark from King George III in 1774, but their fund-raising efforts were interrupted by the outbreak of the American Revolution.

The invasion of Delaware by the British army forced the school to close in 1777, and it was not able to reopen until 1780. In their march through Delaware the British seized both the records and the funds of the Academy of Newark, and though a part of the recently acquired endowment was preserved, the postwar academy was only a rural grammar school, with nothing like its former pretensions.

The trustees were still ambitious of developing their school into a college, but it was to the state, not the Presbyterians, that they now appealed. For years they had no success, as the State of Delaware showed little interest in education. In 1821 friends of the academy in the legislature were surprisingly successful in making the academy the beneficiary, in part, of two new taxes, one on the vendors of foreign goods (as the result of a kind of "buy-American" movement) and the other on stagecoach and steamboat passengers. The people of Delaware were irate about these taxes, and their reaction swept the friends of the academy from the legislature and repealed or amended the tax laws. The academy never realized anything from the stagecoach and steamboat taxes, which were not collected, but some money from a year of taxes on merchants did go to a new College Fund.

The main resource of the College Fund, however, was a lottery, authorized by the state for this purpose. Collected annually for ten years beginning in 1825, the lottery raised sufficient money to allow the academy trustees to contract in 1833 with Winslow Lewis, a Bostonian, to erect a college building, the structure now known as Old College Hall.

To manage their expanded responsibilities and to permit the awarding of college degrees, the trustees sought a new charter from the state legislature. Granted in February 1833, it created a Newark College, incorporating the academy as its preparatory branch, the whole to be governed by a board of trustees that included all the academy trustees plus twice as many more men. In May 1834, after the old academy building had been permanently abandoned, the new institution opened its doors.

Two professors, soon joined by a third, constituted the faculty for this first term. Examining the approximately thirty-five students who applied for admission, they found only one fully prepared for collegiate studies and put all the others in the preparatory branch, though many of these students were promoted to the college after one term. Perhaps because the students were generally ill-prepared, disciplinary problems arose in this first term, leading the trustees to reorganize the institution. Heretofore the chief executive was one of the professors, called the principal, but in the fall of 1834, the board of trustees named the first president of the college.

This man was Eliphalet Wheeler Gilbert, a Presbyterian minister of considerable ability, much learning, and strong opinions. Under his management Newark College prospered, but very shortly he found himself in a moral dilemma. The chief financial support of the school came from a lottery, which the state renewed in 1835 for a second period of ten years. Over the years, Presbyterians had come to believe that lotteries were immoral, and Gilbert concluded that he could not preside over an institution directly supported by such means. His resignation was followed by the resignation of many members of the board of trustees, within which the Presbyterian influence had been dominant since colonial days.

Gilbert's successor was an Episcopal minister, Richard Sharpe Mason, a man of first-rate intellectual qualities but apparently lacking the talent required to manage students. When, after five years, the trustees made known their dissatisfaction with his conduct of the college, Mason resigned. Reversing their previous decision to accept lottery funds, the trustees decided to call Gilbert back to the presidency and to honor his scruples by asking the state to supply the college directly from its revenues in lieu of the lottery funds. The state government agreed to put the lottery receipts into its own treasury and to appropriate an equivalent sum directly to the college. This devious management of the lottery money satisfied Gilbert and he returned to the presidency with the hope of getting further help, both in finances and in the recruitment of students, by emphasizing the Presbyterian connection.

Mason had made several excellent appointments to the faculty, and Gilbert further strengthened that body. To settle some of the problems of student discipline that vexed Mason, the trustees had agreed to remove the preparatory students from the college building. The old academy building was found to be unfit for use, so it was razed and a new building of brick was erected on its site in 1841, with a second building, primarily a dormitory, erected on the same lot to the east of the first building. These buildings are still standing, connected by an addition that was constructed in 1871.

Gilbert's hopes that his Presbyterian connections would help him develop the college into an institution of first rank were disappointed. Enrollments did not grow as he had hoped, and state funds stopped coming to the college in 1845, when the lottery ceased to operate. In 1843 the trustees had the name of the institution changed from Newark College to Delaware College, hoping to draw continued state support. However, Gilbert's concentration on winning support from Presbyterians of several states at the expense of developing connections in Delaware had raised some enemies for the college, enemies who sought to have the charter revoked. After an investigation, the legislature concluded that the college was operated as its charter required, for the benefit of all potential Delaware students regardless of their denominational ties. But the legislators would not vote any further financial assistance to the college.

Unable to sustain college operation from the meager tuition fees collected from students, the trustees began to dip into the endowment, which consisted of so much of the old College Fund, including lottery receipts, as had not been spent on construction and upkeep. Despairing of a future without denominational or state aid, Gilbert resigned in 1847. He was followed in the presidency by a series of men, some quite able but none serving more than three years, while the financial situation of the college became increasingly desperate.

In the early years of the 1850s there was a temporary burst of great optimism about the future of the college, prompted by a new scheme for funding the college through the sale of scholarships, which an agent (a Presbyterian clergyman, of course) was hired to peddle to Presbyterian congregations over a wide area and to men of means of all denominations throughout Delaware. Each person subscribing to the scholarship fund received a certificate with detachable coupons covering tuition costs for one student a year for twenty years or for twenty students in one year; the subscriber could distribute these coupons as he pleased.

Sale of the scholarships seemed to provide a bonanza for the needy college. An immediate influx of funds permitted the hiring of additional faculty, the strengthening of courses, particularly in the sciences and technology, and the improvement of the property, including the addition of a cupola atop Old College Hall. The scholarships brought a great influx of new students, more than at any other time during the nineteenth century, but in a few years it was obvious that a serious miscalculation had occurred. The new funds were spent quickly in meeting the needs of the new students, but even after all of the funds were expended, students continued to arrive with coupons entitling them to free tuition.

Facing an impossible situation, the college authorities began begging scholarship subscribers to give up their certificates as a gift or to sell them back at a discount. To keep going, the trustees each year dipped a bit further into the principal of the college endowment, but the days of the college were clearly numbered. The last hope was an appeal to the state legislature, buttressed by a proposal that the college train teachers for the public schools. Although the idea did win considerable support at the state capitol, it was not sufficient to overcome the reluctance of the state legislators, no longer willing to use lotteries, to raise taxes for benefit either of a college or of the public schools.

At the same time, the public image of the college was seared by a bloody row that led to the murder of a student in Old College Hall. While the incident did not close the college, it threw a pall on its last days. Two more terms passed before the inevitable failure of all resources was acknowledged early in 1859 and the college was closed.

Foiled in their effort to win assistance from the state legislature, the trustees turned once again to the Presbyterians. When these one-time friends of the college decided they already had as many commitments to colleges as they could possibly keep, the

the trustees looked to Episcopalians for succor. But this hope was disappointed as well, and the college remained closed through the troubled decade of the Civil War and the Reconstruction that followed its closing in 1859.

One part of the college, however, had not closed. The preparatory branch, the old academy, had continued to flourish in a modest way. Its enrollments were higher and its costs lower than those of the college, and it still had the use of the old, though small, endowment that was a relic of the colonial institution. In 1869 the academy was formally separated from the defunct college, as a clause in the 1833 college charter permitted. Once again the Academy of Newark was an independent institution, governed under the terms of its Penn charter of 1769.

The separation of the academy from the college resulted from a momentous development in the history of the latter—its designation as the land-grant college of the State of Delaware. In 1862 the Congress of the United States had enacted the Land-Grant College Act (also called the Morrill Act), which provided federal aid to every state for use by colleges that featured training in agriculture and mechanic arts, and military science, as well as other subjects. In selecting Delaware College, a private institution, the state legislature had little choice. The Morrill Act had ordered that none of the land-grant funds could be spent on buidings. If the state had desired to start a new, entirely public institution, it would have faced the expense of constructing or buying a college building. The trustees of Delaware College offered an existing, if inoperative, institution to undertake the responsibilities set out in the Morrill Act, and there was no other college in Delaware that was so likely a choice. Furthermore, the trustees agreed to amend their charter so as to cede one-half of all college property to the state and to permit the governor to name one-half of the members of the board.

The original Morrill Act did not bring great wealth to Delaware College. Delaware's income from land-grant aid amounted to only $4,980 a year, and even though $1,000 was then a sufficient annual salary to attract a professor, this income was not enough to provide for faculty, upkeep, and supplies for a college. Moreover,

almost all Delaware students were to receive free tuition (as part
of the deal with the state), and there were few out-of-state applicants. Yet, notwithstanding the financial pressures, the trustees
dared to reopen the college in the fall of 1870, with one of their
own members as president, William H. Purnell, an alumnus who
was well known in his native Maryland as a lawyer and a poli-
tician. Two years later Purnell persuaded the trustees to admit
women as well as men. There were no dormitory facilities for
women, so the enrollment of coeds was limited to students who
could live at home or with friends or relatives in town or could
board at the academy, which soon became coeducational.

Purnell sought to identify the college with the state and particularly with the public schools. He became president of the state
board of education and successfully pleaded with the legislature in
1873 for a grant of money to begin a program of teacher education.
Student literary societies, dating to the origins of the college, were
revived; through lectures and debates, publications, and especially
libraries, they furnished a very valuable addition to classroom
studies. Organized athletics were begun, as were student publications; the student newspaper, the *Review,* issued its first number
in 1882.

Financially the college could only limp along. The state appro-
priation for teacher training was not renewed after expiration of a
two-year period. A science curriculum, including engineering,
proved attractive, but students could not be persuaded to take
more than a smattering of work in agriculture. Total enrollments
remained low (seldom much beyond fifty students) despite the
admission of women—or because of it, according to some critics of
coeducation among both the trustees and the student body.

Dissatisfaction with both President Purnell and coeducation
(attacked especially on the grounds that women should not be
permitted to take courses in a building that was also a men's
dormitory) gradually mounted. In the spring of 1885, Purnell resigned and the trustees immediately abolished coeducation, though
allowing those women already enrolled to complete their courses.

Purnell's successor as president, John Hollis Caldwell, an elderly Methodist minister who had won some local fame (and some notoriety) in Georgia after the Civil War, turned out to be a disaster. Though in Georgia he had been known as a radical because of his support of the rights of the black freedmen, especially their right to an education, he was an ultra-conservative in his attitude toward student conduct at college. Opposing plays and dances on campus, he became involved in a feud with the faculty that finally led to his resignation after three years. By that time Caldwell's management had almost closed the college, which was reduced to sixteen students in the spring of 1888.

His successor, Albert N. Raub, was a professional educator who won the attention of the trustees by his success as principal of the Academy of Newark. Raub quickly increased enrollment, though to do so he reduced entrance requirements drastically. Besides enjoying invigorated administration, the college profited by federal legislation (the Hatch Act) establishing an agricultural experiment station and by a second Morrill Act, which brought additional annual federal funds to support the teaching of not only agriculture and engineering, but also the sciences, mathematics, economics, and English. Never thereafter was the college in such desperate financial straits as it had known prior to 1889.

At approximately the same time, the state legislature began assisting the college. With state aid, Old College Hall had been enlarged in 1885–1886, and in the next twenty years state funds permitted construction of new classroom and laboratory buildings. Raub resigned the presidency in 1896; he was succeeded by George A. Harter, professor of mathematics, whose eighteen-year administration was the second longest in the college's history. Harter's presidency was a period of unspectacular, but slow and steady progress. The engineering program proved so popular that it overshadowed older programs in the arts and sciences, with civil engineering decidedly the leading study. Research, hitherto dependent on the personal initiative of faculty members, was given emphasis and prestige by federal support for agriculture. After the appointment of Harry Hayward as director of the experiment station in 1906 (and later as the first dean), this field of study, hitherto unpopular with students, began to attract reasonable enrollments. A second experimental farm located just south of Newark was purchased, and much of the first farm, adjacent to the campus, was converted into an athletic field, named for Joseph H. Frazer, a graduate whose heirs perpetuated his memory by financing the development of the facility.

Progress on the campus led the legislature to make increasingly frequent gifts to addresss specific needs of the college until 1909, when it began to make annual grants toward upkeep of the enlarged college property as well as specific grants to support the study of state history and government. Finally, in 1913, the long neglect of women's education was ended with passage of legislation creating a Women's College.

The Women's College Act culminated a well-organized campaign directed primarily by Emalea P. Warner, wife of a Wilmington industrialist. Presidents Caldwell and Raub had favored admission of women to Delaware College, but had been unable to overcome existing prejudice against coeducation. Mrs. Warner, acting on behalf of the State Federation of Women's Clubs, but also aided by such other groups as the State Grange, the Women's Christian Temperance Union, the Equal Suffrage Association, and a committee of college women (forerunner of the American Association of University Women), worked out with President Harter, Dean Hayward, and others representing Delaware College, a proposal that better suited the current attitudes of Delawareans. This proposal was for a coordinate women's college that would be located near Delaware College so as to make use of some of its faculty, but would be a college for women only, with some administrators and some faculty of its own. It would follow the model of the women's colleges established at several Eastern institutions, including Brown, Columbia, and Harvard, rejecting adoption of the thoroughgoing coeducational system characteristic of Western state universities—and of Delaware from 1872 to 1885.

The state purchased a new campus for the Women's College one-half mile south of the Delaware College campus (midway between it and the farm) and began the erection of two structures, a dormitory and a classroom building. A dean was appointed to organize and open the new college, and the choice was remarkably fortunate. Once appointed dean, Winifred Josephine Robinson, previously an assistant professor of botany at Vassar, moved to Newark in March 1914 and began to recruit staff and students for a fall opening. Dean Robinson and Mrs. Warner, who made a compatible team, traveled throughout the state urging high school girls to apply to the new college, and when it opened in September 1914 the fifty-eight students who enrolled were more than most friends of the Women's College had dared hope for.

Meanwhile, new life was stirring at old Delaware College. A group of alumni, led by W. O. Sypherd, a professor of English, and H. Rodney Sharp, a close associate of Pierre S. du Pont, who was his brother-in-law, had concluded that the college for men was not progressing as it could and should. President Harter, like other presidents before him, was busy as a teaching member of the faculty and could give only part of his time to administrative duties. The great need, this group of alumni thought, was for a full-time president who could concentrate on college problems and development without being distracted by the demands of the classroom.

Raising money privately for the purpose, these alumni provided the means for hiring Samuel Chiles Mitchell, an historian who was then president of the Medical College of Virginia and who had previously served in the same capacity at the University of South Carolina. Hardly had Mitchell arrived in Newark when he was told that Pierre S. du Pont, who was becoming increasingly eager to improve public education in Delaware, had resolved to give Delaware College a million dollars over a period of a few years. As these funds (given anonymously for the most part) became available, the campus was extended by purchase of all the land between Main Street and the Women's College, new buildings were constructed, Old College was wholly refurbished (though the old exterior was preserved), and some money went into funds for upkeep and for salaries. Among curricular developments were the beginning of teacher-training programs in secondary education (available to both sexes, though in separate classes) and in elementary education (open only to women). A summer school, primarily for teachers, which had been initiated in 1913, became a valuable means of extending assistance to teachers in service.

American entry in the First World War briefly interrupted the renascence of Delaware College. In 1918 practically all male students were mustered into the Student Army Reserve Corps; while their programs of study were hardly affected, they lived under military regimen. Additional room had to be found on campus for soldiers on active duty who were sent to Newark for specific training of various sorts.

President Mitchell was very active as a committee member and lecturer on the national scene in endeavors connected with the war effort (he had three sons in uniform) and with such varied purposes as postwar world peace, interracial harmony, Christian youth movements, and the diffusion of education to all peoples. He loved the lecture platform and decided finally that he wished to devote his remaining years to teaching history and to efforts to improve education in his native South. He acted on this decision in 1920 by resigning to return to a professorship at the University of Richmond, where he had enjoyed teaching earlier in his career.

To his place the trustees appointed another Southerner, Walter Hullihen, who came to Newark from a deanship at the University of the South (Sewanee) to begin the longest presidential term in Delaware's history. One of Hullihen's first steps, in 1921, was to have the charter amended so that the institution henceforth would be named the University of Delaware. Since there were now two colleges, the new title clarified an organizational structure that had been confusing since 1914, when the Women's College had opened as a unit subject to the authority of the president and trustees of Delaware College.

Another important innovation in the early years of the Hullihen administration was the Delaware Foreign Study Plan, known as the Junior Year Abroad program. The inspiration of a young assistant professor of French, Raymond Kirkbride, this plan was directed at embellishing the education of undergraduate advanced students of French by allowing them to spend their junior year at the University of Paris and receive a full year's credit for work done there toward baccalaureate degrees at Delaware. Heretofore many Americans had gone abroad for graduate study, but Kirkbride wished to provide experience abroad for an ordinary college undergraduate, such a person as might plan on a career in business, in which knowledge of foreign countries and their cultures was seriously lacking. Founded in 1923, the Delaware Junior Year Abroad program was soon followed by the establishment of similar programs, notably at Smith College in Massachusetts and since World War II also at numerous colleges and universities throughout the nation (though discontinued at Delaware in 1948).

Of more permanent benefit to the university was President Hullihen's campaign for a new library. Planned as a memorial to the men of the state who had died in World War I, the library was constructed in 1924 after a statewide fund drive. Thousands of school children as well as numerous adults contributed, but the greatest assistance came as a gift from Pierre S. du Pont and from the efforts of H. Rodney Sharp, who helped manage the campaign and paid all of its costs.

Sharp was also donor of an auditorium, Mitchell Hall, named for the former president, and state funds provided for several other buildings, including a women's gym and dining hall and an engineering building (Evans Hall). Throughout the Hullihen years, however, state appropriations remained so small that there was little financial leeway to upgrade the quality of the school (in terms of salaries and library books, for instance) to match the beautiful campus that special gifts and appropriations made possible.

The Depression negated the possibility of additional state contributions for new buildings or programs. On the contrary, appropriations to the university were temporarily reduced and so were salaries. But the state of the national job market for university professors somewhat relieved the problem of retaining good faculty, and for extraordinary needs a new benefactor emerged in the person of H. Fletcher Brown, a former Du Pont Company official who devoted his retirement years to the improvement of public education in Delaware, especially at the university. Brown's gifts, complemented in some cases by the federal public works program, made possible construction of a chemical laboratory, a classroom-administration building, a dormitory, and an extensive enlargement of the Memorial Library, as well as more construction after his death and a very sizable addition to the hitherto small endowment. Brown also helped the university strengthen what had been a mediocre chemical engineering program, primarily by the addition in 1939 of a new chairman, Allan Colburn, along with support for research that Colburn inaugurated.

World War II turned out to be a watershed in the university's history. Most of the male students left to join the armed forces in 1943, and a considerable part of the faculty did likewise or entered war work as civilians. Soldiers and young reserves sent to the campus in the Army Specialized Training Program (or the Army Specialized Training Reserve Program) kept the numbers of students at the university close to the previous level, but civilian men were so few in number that by special permission they were allowed to enter classes consisting mainly of women. This proved to be a step toward the adoption of coeducation, which had been made possible before the war when, upon Dean Robinson's retirement in 1938, the trustees granted permission to merge small classes of men and women in the final two undergraduate years. Summer school classes, which had become increasingly popular for undergraduates who were seeking to make up deficiencies or to graduate early, were always coeducational.

The sudden death of Walter Hullihen in 1944 brought to the presidency Professor W. O. Sypherd, an advocate of coeducation, who quickly procured trustee approval of a wholesale reorganization, abolishing both Delaware College and the Women's College as separate entities and advancing the programs in education and in home economics to the status of schools, ranking with those of arts and science, engineering, and agriculture.

When Sypherd, who was close to retirement age, refused the permanent presidency, William Samuel Carlson, a Midwesterner, was brought to Newark in 1946 as the new president. Enrollments suddenly surged when veterans, supported by the G.I. Bill, entered the university. Quickly, student numbers grew to more than twice what they had been before the war, when there were never quite one thousand students. The state legislature, grateful to the veterans who were thronging to college, increased appropriations to meet campus needs, and private benefactors also contributed to the university's growth.

During the war the chemical engineering department, under Allan Colburn's dynamic leadership and by means of his splendid national reputation, had become a center of research. This department's leadership was recognized soon after the war when it was permitted, in June 1948, to award the first earned doctorate in University of Delaware history. The chemistry department, upgraded to keep pace with chemical engineering, was also granted permission to award the Ph.D. degree and did so for the first time in September 1948.

That year, 1948, also marked another milestone in the history of the university. Before then, racial segregation, which was rooted in Delaware's history as a slave state prior to the Civil War, had been practiced at the college level and in the public schools. Under pressure from Congress to make provision for black students, the state legislature had founded Delaware State College in 1891 and assigned it a share of the Morrill Act funds because blacks were not admitted to Delaware College. In 1948, in response to recent decisions by federal courts, the board of trustees opened the university to black students in programs not offered at Delaware State, including engineering and graduate studies.

The trustees thought this was as far as they could go in view of the segregation enforced by law in the public schools. In 1950, however, a group of students at Delaware State College successfully brought suit for admission to the University of Delaware on the grounds that Delaware State College did not offer programs of equal quality to those at the university. The decision of this suit in Delaware chancery court immediately opened the university to all Delaware students, whatever their race or color, and very soon all restrictions against black students from out of state were removed.

In the year of the chancery court decision, a new president, John A. Perkins, began a seventeen-year term. Thirty-six when he came to Newark—the youngest president in the institution's history—Perkins gave vigorous leadership at a time when the state and the university were undergoing rapid growth. In the 1950s Delaware underwent by far its most rapid population growth (by over forty percent) since before the American Revolution. And from an undergraduate student population of 1,500 in 1951, the university grew to 2,400 in 1957-58, and then more rapidly to 3,600 in 1961-62 and 6,500 in 1967-68.

Graduate enrollments and programs also increased through these years. An average of twenty Ph.D.s were awarded in the years just prior to 1963, but in 1967 the number of doctorates granted mounted to fifty. By the latter year there were over seven hundred graduate students engaged in full-time campus studies; many more students carried on part-time graduate work.

The rapid growth in enrollment that characterized the latter years of the Perkins administration continued during the acting-presidency of John W. Shirley (1967-68) and in the early years of the presidency of E. Arthur Trabant, which began in 1968. By 1974 there were 12,577 undergraduates enrolled, and by 1976 the undergraduate enrollment had exceeded 13,000. In the next few years, however, in keeping with national trends and partly in response to a lower birth rate, enrollment leveled off.

The unpopular Vietnam War and the military draft led to a period of great student unrest from about 1966 to 1970. Student rallies, protests, and petitions became the order of the day. Among the concessions made to student demands was the abolition (in 1968) of the requirement of military training that had been imposed in 1870. All attempts to enforce dress codes were abandoned, residence rules were liberalized (and coed dorms introduced), and some specific course requirements were abandoned.

As a counter to a spirit of divisiveness that had arisen within the university, the new Trabant administration in 1968 sought to provide various elements of the university body with opportunities to influence policy making. Students were placed on many committees and invited to participate in formulating what was called a community design for the growth of each segment of the institution. And a faculty senate was established, largely composed of elective members, which effectively undertook responsibilities that the faculty, as it rapidly grew larger, had been neglecting.

A special study of the needs of minority students, completed in 1969, led to the establishment of a minorities center and of a department of black American studies. Efforts were also made to recruit increasing numbers of black students, faculty, and staff. Women's interests on campus were also given special attention. Sororities, long banned by choice of a majority of women students, were permitted to organize on campus in 1966 and in 1969 women athletes were allowed to engage in intercollegiate competition. The proportion of women in the student body steadily mounted until it became a majority in the 1970s.

Increasing enrollments in the 1950s and 1960s necessitated expansion of the campus and construction of more dormitories, laboratory and classroom buildings, and athletic facilities. It also led to the expansion of academic programs, including establishment in 1962 of a School of Business and Economics, which grew so rapidly that in less than two decades it became the university's second largest college—the new title given to all of the existing schools in 1965. In 1966, the department of nursing, which had been created after World War II, was also raised to college status. A graduate program in early American material culture, undertaken in 1952 in cooperation with the Winterthur Museum founded by Henry Francis du Pont, a university trustee, very soon became the leading program in America for the training of museum directors and curators. It also served as a model for other graduate programs undertaken with the Hagley Museum (featuring business and industrial history) and with Longwood Gardens (affording training in management of botanical gardens), as well as a program in art conservation that was offered in collaboration with Winterthur. These special programs were complemented in 1972 by a certificate program in museum studies available to all qualified graduate students; these programs helped to solidify the high reputation the university had gained in training for museum careers.

For undergraduates, new or expanded courses were offered in such fields as communications (which absorbed courses offered earlier in speech), computer sciences, geology, and several of the social sciences. A program in medical technology was introduced soon after the war; courses in criminal justice later became a popular feature of the sociology department.

During the Trabant administration, three new colleges were opened. Two of them, the College of Marine Studies (1970) and the College of Urban Affairs and Public Policy (1971) catered exclusively to graduate students, while the College of Physical Education, Athletics, and Recreation (1980) offered both undergraduate and graduate programs. Decentralization of graduate studies led to abandonment of a separate graduate college, but graduate programs continued to increase. Such programs became particularly important to the College of Education, where about forty percent of the students were taking graduate courses by 1982. Meanwhile, the College of Home Economics, which had enlarged its focus, had its new responsibilities recognized in 1978 when its name was changed to the College of Human Resources. An Honors Program initiated in 1976 attracted many superior students to the university and, now offering more than one hundred enriched or intensified courses in over thirty disciplines each semester to students throughout the university, has been recognized as one of the leading honors programs in the nation. In addition, an Office of Women's Affairs was established in 1978 in response to the increasing role of women in all aspects of university life.

The need for additional classroom buildings caused the same sort of campus expansion as the need for dormitories. One especially notable new building was the Hugh M. Morris Library (1963). Support for the new buildings came from federal and state governments and from bond issues, along with gifts from private individuals and foundations. Through the years following World War II, the university was the fortunate recipient of many private benefactions. Notable among them was a large annual gift received as the income of a trust fund diverted by H. Rodney Sharp from

1950 until his death in 1968 to the institution for which he had already proved a loyal supporter. The estate of Amy du Pont, who died in 1962, endowed the Unidel Foundation, which she had established in 1939 and which made grants to support special projects at the university. Judge Hugh M. Morris, a university alumnus and chairman of the board of trustees from 1939 to 1959, helped set up the Unidel Foundation and eventually left his own sizable estate to the university.

As its private resources increased, the university successfully sought an amendment of its charter, granted by the legislature in 1964, freeing it from supervision by state authorities for any except the state-funded portion of its income. The state connection, however, remained strong, since the governor and the president of the state board of education remained *ex officio* members of the board of trustees, to which the governor appointed eight members to six-year terms. These eight trustees, plus twenty who were elected by the full board, were subject to confirmation by the state senate.

Private gifts, including subventions from industry and foundations, helped the university to progress as a research center. Harry Haskell and others founded what became the University of Delaware Research Foundation, a basis for the funding of scientific research by young scholars on the faculty. An Institute for Energy Conversion, quartered eventually in a building erected specifically for its needs, carried on research focused on photovoltaic cells. Other research organizations, some of them interdepartmental, proliferated, including the Center for Composite Materials, the Center for Catalytic Science and Technology, the Institute of Applied Mathematics, and the Bartol Foundation, which moved its offices from Swarthmore to Newark to work in close collaboration with the physics department.

The oldest organized research in the university was connected with the agricultural programs. Additional experimental farms were acquired downstate, notably a substation outside Georgetown. The cooperative extension service, directed from the university campus, employed county agents and other staff members in each county. A major beneficial insects laboratory of the United

States Department of Agriculture was moved from Moorestown, New Jersey, to Newark in 1973.

Besides the agricultural substation at Georgetown, another university facility in Sussex County developed at Lewes, where the College of Marine Studies moored its craft and carried on research in a variety of buildings. Similarly, the university extended its work to Wilmington, where it established an office for an urban agent and acquired two properties, Wilcastle and Goodstay, the latter (by gift of Robert and Ellen du Pont Wheelwright) as a conference center and the former as a home for the large number of classes being conducted for adults at night by the Office of Continuing Education. Wilcastle also proved a useful facility for the Academy of Lifelong Learning, which operates a similar program of noncredit courses directed to the interests of retired men and women.

By 1980 the University of Delaware offered a diverse student body the opportunity for full- and part-time study in 105 undergraduate majors, 80 fields for the master's degree, and 40 for the doctorate. The size and complexity of institutional affairs were a far cry from those of the plain academy opened by Francis Alison outside New London in 1743 or the college chartered in 1833, which admitted its first students in 1834.

Contributors

JAN H. BLITS, associate professor of educational and political philosophy at the University of Delaware, is the author of *The End of the Ancient Republic: Essays on Shakespeare's "Julius Caesar"* and has contributed numerous articles to philosophical and political science journals. His most recent publication is "Privacy and Moral Education: Aristotle's Critique of the Family" (*Educational Theory*, 1985).

C. HAROLD BROWN is vice-president for personnel and employee relations at the University of Delaware and former dean of the College of Urban Affairs and Public Policy. He has been president of the Urban Affairs Association and has published widely in sociology and policy journals, with particular interest in youth migration and neighborhood centers.

ERIC BRUCKER, dean of the College of Business and Economics at the University of Delaware, has served as president of the Middle Atlantic Association of Colleges of Business Administration. His current research deals with the determinants of productivity growth in the United States.

ALAN MCCLELLAND, assistant to the director of the Central Research and Development Department of the E. I. DuPont de Ne-

Nemours Company, has been a research chemist in universities and in industry. He has taught at the University of Connecticut and is current chairman of the American Chemical Society's committee on education.

JOHN A. MUNROE, H. Rodney Sharp Professor Emeritus of History at the University of Delaware, is the author of *Federalist Delaware, 1775-1815* and *Louis McLane, Federalist and Jacksonian.*

FRANK B. MURRAY, H. Rodney Sharp Professor and dean of the College of Education at the University of Delaware, is a member of the board of directors and former president of the Jean Piaget Society. He has edited several books on educational psychology, is a frequent contributor to scholarly journals, and is editor of *The Genetic Epistemologist* as well as associate editor of the *American Educational Research Journal.*

DAVID S. SAXON is chairman of the Corporation, Massachusetts Institute of Technology. He is a former president, and provost of the University of California. His publications include *Elementary Quantum Mechanics, The Nuclear Independent Particle Model, Discontinuities in Wave Guides, Physics for the Liberal Arts Student,* and numerous journal articles on physics. He is a fellow of the American Academy of Arts and Sciences and of the American Physical Society.

HOWARD E. SIMMONS, JR., vice-president of the Central Research and Development Department of the E. I. DuPont de Nemours Company, is a member of the American Academy of Arts and Sciences and the National Academy of Science. He has been Sloan Visiting Professor at Harvard University, Karasch Visiting Professor at the University of Chicago, and adjunct professor of chemistry at the University of Delaware. He has published numerous papers in scientific journals and is on the editorial boards of *Synthesis* and the *Journal of Organic Chemistry.*

JOHN B. SLAUGHTER, chancellor of the University of Maryland, College Park, is former director of the National Science Foundation and academic vice-president and provost of Washington State University. He has served on the National Research Council's committee on minorities in engineering and on the National Science Board's committee on pre-college education. He has published extensively in scientific journals and is editor of the *Journal of Computers and Electrical Engineering*.

VIRGINIA B. SMITH, president of Vassar College, has served as director of the Fund for Improvement of Postsecondary Education and as president of the board of the Society for Values in Higher Education. She is a member of the board of directors of the Carnegie Foundation for the Advancement of Teaching and a member of the National Commission on Higher Education Issues. She is coauthor of *The Impersonal Campus* and a contributor to *Universal Higher Education: Costs and Benefits, Recurrent Education*, and *Education and the State*.

LINDA TOM is director of employee relations at the University of Delaware. She has served as assistant director of the Delaware Public Administration Institute of the University of Delaware's College of Urban Affairs and Public Policy.

E. ARTHUR TRABANT, president of the University of Delaware, is former vice-president for academic affairs at Georgia Tech and dean of the School of Engineering at the State University of New York at Buffalo. He has taught at Purdue University, where he also served as assistant dean of the Graduate School and head of the Division of Engineering Science. He has contributed many articles to engineering and mathematics journals.

RICHARD L. VENEZKY, Unidel Professor of Educational Studies and Computer Sciences at the University of Delaware, has been chairman of the Department of Computer Sciences at the University of

Wisconsin. His publications include *A Microfiche Concordance to Old English, Letter and Word Perception, The Structure of English Orthography*, and numerous articles on reading as well as computers and the humanities. He is a consultant to the *Oxford English Dictionary Supplement* and is a member of the editorial boards of *Computers and the Humanities, Human Learning*, and *Cognition and Learning*.